Loss and bereavement

Health psychology

Series editors:
Sheila Payne and Sandra Horn

Published titles

Stress: Perspectives and Processes
Dean Bartlett

Psychology and Health Promotion
Paul Bennett and Simon Murphy

The Social Context of Health
Michael Hardey

Pain: Theory, Research and Intervention
Sandra Horn and Marcus Munafò

Loss and Bereavement
Sheila Payne, Sandra Horn and Marilyn Relf

Loss and bereavement

**Sheila Payne, Sandra Horn
and Marilyn Relf**

Open University Press
Buckingham · Philadelphia

Open University Press
Celtic Court
22 Ballmoor
Buckingham
MK18 1XW

e-mail: enquiries@openup.co.uk
world wide web: http://www.openup.co.uk

and

325 Chestnut Street
Philadelphia, PA 19106, USA

First Published 1999

A catalogue record of this book is available from the British Library

ISBN   0 335 20105 9 (pb)   0 335 20106 7 (hb)

Library of Congress Cataloging-in-Publication Data
Payne, Sheila, 1954–
    Loss and bereavement / Sheila Payne, Sandra Horn, Marilyn Relf.
      p.   cm. – (Health psychology)
    Includes bibliographical references and index.
    ISBN 0–335–20106–7 (hardcover). – ISBN 0–335–20105–9 (pbk.)
    1. Bereavement–Psychological aspects.   2. Loss (Psychology)
3. Grief.   4. Death–Psychological aspects.   I. Horn. Sandra.
II. Relf, Marilyn.   III. Title.   IV. Series.
BF575.G7P3775 1999
155.9'37–dc21   99–24181
                                                                                          CIP

Typeset by Graphicraft Ltd, Hong Kong
Printed in Great Britain by Biddles Ltd, Guildford and King's Lynn

# Contents

Series editors' foreword

This series of books in health psychology is designed to support postgraduate and postqualification studies in psychology, nursing, medicine and paramedical sciences, as well as the establishment of health psychology within the undergraduate psychology curriculum. Health psychology is growing rapidly as a field of study. Concerned as it is with the application of psychological theories and models in the promotion and maintenance of health, and the individual and interpersonal aspects of adaptive behaviour in illness and disability, health psychology has a wide remit and an important role to play in the future.

This book aims to give students an understanding of important theoretical perspectives and specific models of adaptation to loss. The authors have made the assumption that loss and change are normal processes which occur within a social and cultural context. The book critically examines the complex nature of loss and shows how differing theoretical positions have commented on the relationships between the bereaved and the deceased. It is a timely contribution to the literature which has moved from global phase or stage models of understanding loss to more integrative models in which individual variability is recognized. There remains debate as to what constitutes 'resolution' of grief and how this is achieved, over what time span, and by what processes. The authors draw on a wide variety of sources and disciplinary perspectives including historical accounts, anthropology, sociology, psychiatry and psychology. They offer critical explanations of relevant theories and suggest how these impact on practical issues such as bereavement support services. The book is a scholarly account of concepts of loss and bereavement which draws together and discusses recent developments within the field.

Sheila Payne and Sandra Horn

Introduction

It is evident that death and grief are too multisplendoured and complex to be trussed up in the conceptual straitjacket of any one discipline.

(Feifel 1998: 4)

This book is about loss, and specifically about how we investigate and attempt to understand the impact of loss by death on individuals, families and larger social groups on the one hand, and how individual and group factors shape our experience of loss on the other.

In past times, in many cultures, dying, death and bereavement were the province of the family, neighbours and priests or their equivalent. In some cultures, tasks such as laying out the corpse or keening over the body were undertaken by certain specialists who were usually paid for their services – this is still true in many countries of the world – but they were typically members of the community and known to the family. Today, in much of the western world, death and the issues surrounding it have become professionalized and may incorporate the services of nurses, doctors, undertakers, psychologists and counsellors among others. The implications of these changes are among the issues we will consider in this book. Perhaps it is to the institutionalization of dying and death that we owe the development of the science of thanatology, whose scholars seek to explore and describe the issues in order to enhance our understanding and, it is to be hoped, our management of them.

That the study of bereavement and its associated phenomena is now an established subdiscipline of the psychosocial and clinical sciences is fitting for a topic which is both universal and deeply significant in human experience. The impact of significant loss by death results in the need for adaptation at both individual and group levels, and the process of such adaptation may be prolonged and painful. The means by which individuals and groups manage and contain the impact of bereavement, and the social and individual constructions of the 'right' and 'wrong' ways to accomplish the necessary adaptation are proving to be complex and demanding areas of study.

In the field of health, researchers and clinicians have noted the morbidity and mortality and the physical and psychosocial disturbances that accompany grief. There are problems in the terminology and definition of grief that appears to 'go wrong'; this may be variously referred to as abnormal, pathological, complicated or difficult grief. In this book we have used all these terms and they should not be taken to infer any value judgements on our part. We are aware of the debates in the literature and have chosen not to take sides, but we have explained in the text the implications of these terms and why some may be preferable to others. In particular, there has been objection to the use of the terms abnormal and pathological, because they imply that there is a 'normal' way to *do* bereavement. Moreover, these terms are closely associated with psychiatric and medical models of understanding, and some researchers wish to distance themselves from these models. We would argue that there is variability in patterns of grieving, and some of this variability gives cause for concern either in the bereaved or those who interact with them. Identifying the factors which determine outcome is by no means easy, particularly as the boundaries of normal and abnormal, healthy and morbid, vary through history and across cultures.

Feifel (1998: 3) points out that 'grief is multifaceted and manifests numerous faces . . . the line between healthy and unhealthy grief, at times, can get blurred and difficult to distinguish. An instructive criterion in this respect seems to be that unhealthy grief may reveal itself in deviant behaviour that violates conventional expectations or imperils the health and safety of self and others'. While the latter point made by Feifel is unarguable, the notion of violating conventional expectations as a marker of abnormality is contentious: in societies where the conventions are unhelpful and unhealthy, there may be a need to grieve in unconventional ways, and sometimes this need forces change, as, it may be argued, is happening in Britain at the time of writing. This topic will be pursued further in Chapter 2. Describing and predicting those intra- and inter-individual factors which facilitate adaptation to loss, and identifying those which will inhibit or distort the process is, then, a growing area of concern in this the latter half of the twentieth century, but is not without its share of conceptual difficulties. In an attempt to address and elucidate the core issues, we have drawn on a range of contemporary models and research – for example on stress and coping, family dynamics and cross-cultural studies.

Interest in *how* people grieve has been paralleled by interest in *when* they grieve. Models of grief such as phase theory have been applied to a range of situations involving losses or 'exits', including abortion, unemployment, relationship breakdown, and loss of a body part or function. This has led to the use of interventions derived from work on grief. The wide application of models which have not yet been convincingly demonstrated in the field for which they were devised – bereavement – is problematic, as will be argued later, but on the other hand it has also served to focus attention on the fact that these transitions may also involve painful adaptation, and are deserving of study in their own right.

We have here brought together historical and cultural accounts of human-kind's attempts to come to terms with death and its aftermath, together with research and writings on the development of models of loss and contemporary concepts. Thus, although the focus of this book is health psychology, in order to explore concepts around loss and grief fully, we have drawn on disciplines and approaches as diverse as archaeology, anthropology, history, sociology, medicine and psychology, and the perspectives we have sampled range from societal to individual, from experimental to clinical. There will, of course, always be more to tell than can or should be contained within the pages of one small book, but our intention is to introduce the key areas in research and writings on loss, in the hope that our readers will read on, and widely.

We have concentrated on theory and research related to adult experiences of loss. We have sought to offer the reader a variety of theoretical perspectives and suggest how their strengths and weaknesses have influenced our thinking and the design of research. How children experience loss and bereavement is an important issue which is worthy of a book in its own right. Therefore we have only briefly mentioned relevant theories and research related to children.

Each chapter is introduced by a brief account of its contents, and each ends with a summary and recommendations for further reading. Material is cross-referenced throughout the book, and there is a common list of references, but each chapter can also be read as a stand-alone unit of learning.

Chapter 1 starts by defining the key terminology, including bereavement, grief and mourning. It introduces the concept of loss by addressing questions such as the following:

◆ What do we mean by loss? Loss involves more than just the death of a person – it can involve changes in social roles and expectations, changes in body image and function.
◆ Are there commonalities in the experience of loss across cultures? Anthropological research is drawn on to illustrate specific cultural influences such as the 'bright face' of the Balinese.
◆ To what extent do mourning rituals change during the course of history? It could be argued that mourning behaviours and rituals reflect the mores of each society and are in keeping with their time in history. For example, we have highlighted one episode during which there was significant loss of life (the First World War and its aftermath) to discuss the influence of national events on historical transitions in mourning practices.
◆ Can you lose something you never had, such as anticipated roles or dreams of parenthood, marriage or promotion? For example, we discuss emerging Japanese rituals designed to help people cope with the grief and loss associated with the use of surgical abortion as a mechanism of birth control.

The chapter deals with the findings from research and historical accounts without reference to the type of loss, but sets death, dying and bereavement in a social, cultural and historical context. It emphasizes collective responses and takes a macro level of analysis.

Chapter 2 explores the concept of loss from an individual perspective. The reader is introduced to the impact of loss on the individual, in terms of physical, psychological, sexual and spiritual functioning. It examines how the burden of grief is expressed in physical and psychological pain and distress, and what relationship grief has with subsequent health. It reviews the epidemiological evidence of health consequences – the mortality and morbidity – associated with bereavement and addresses the following questions:

♦ Do bereaved people die of a broken heart?
♦ Does the stress of bereavement precipitate or potentiate illness?
♦ What are the possible mechanisms for the effects of loss on an individual's health?

The chapter concludes by introducing a major theoretical perspective on loss – stress and coping, and debates the value of this approach to understanding loss.

In Chapter 3, the focus is on the family and the impact of loss on family systems. The chapter considers the extent to which loss can be understood in terms of disruptions to normal social relationships. Social support is generally perceived to be a helpful strategy for buffering the adverse effects of loss but the research evidence suggests that not all people perceive support to be helpful in bereavement and not everyone can elicit the types of support that they need. The relevance of family systems theories to loss and bereavement are reviewed. The studies reviewed point the way for more research with a broader range of people, experiencing different types of loss.

Chapters 4 and 5 are closely linked. In Chapter 4, we ask questions about how different deaths are perceived depending upon their nature and when they occur in the life cycle, and in particular consider 'untimely' deaths such as those at the very beginning of life – for example, miscarriage, still birth and neonatal loss. We ask:

♦ What impact do these deaths have on the individuals involved, and how are they marked by society?
♦ Why do the rituals following these deaths differ from adult death rituals?

The majority of Chapter 4 focuses on introducing theoretical approaches based on life span, developmental and psychosocial transition perspectives. We introduce the theoretical ideas which underpin the models proposed by Freud, Bowlby, Parkes and Marris. These writers have been hugely influential in determining how loss and bereavement are conceptualized in the twentieth century.

Chapter 5 then presents detailed accounts of the phase models of loss, especially the work of Bowlby and Parkes. We review developments in conceptual models over the last 30 years, including the work of Kulber-Ross and Worden. These models are evaluated, drawing on the critiques in the literature, to examine the different assumptions that underpin ideas such as the 'grief work' hypothesis. The chapter concludes by debating a number of new theoretical developments in the field, including the Dual Process Model of Stroebe and her colleagues, the biographical model proposed by Walter and the hypothesis of continuing relationships with the deceased expounded by Klass and his colleagues.

The book concludes with a final chapter devoted to discussing how best to help bereaved people. We demonstrate how the previously introduced models have been influential in guiding notions of the parameters of 'normal' and 'abnormal' grief and defining the purpose of interventions. While we review the advantages of these approaches, we also highlight dangers such as the potential to pathologize or medicalize the normal processes of grief, and the disempowerment this might entail. In addition, we comment on how pervasive expectations of phases (stages) of grief have become among health professionals and other social care workers, and the possible outcomes of this. Foucault (1973) identified the 'clinical gaze' by which medicine focuses its interests on the objectified body. More recently, May (1992) has suggested the term 'therapeutic gaze' in relation to a focus on the 'mind' of the person (or patient). With the growth of bereavement counselling and support services, there is an increased emphasis on the psychological surveillance of the bereaved. We consider three different types of bereavement services: professional, volunteer and self-help. Clearly, undertaking this type of work, in whatever capacity, places heavy demands of the psychological resources of individuals. The literature on burnout and occupational stress arising from dealing with intensely personal and distressing encounters on a daily basis is discussed. The chapter concludes with a description of research designed to evaluate the efficacy of interventions, highlighting both what is known and not yet known about how to design, deliver and evaluate such services.

This book has been written by authors with backgrounds in health psychology, clinical psychology, bereavement services management and nursing. We have attempted to present the current theoretical debates in a manner which will engage and interest the reader. We are also active researchers, so are well aware of both the limits to our knowledge base and those more generally in the bereavement field. It is an exciting area, with a wealth of complex and insightful theories, and still many challenging questions to be addressed. Finally, we have drawn on our own experiences of personally meaningful losses to understand this topic. We hope that readers will become engaged with these theoretical debates, and that some will seek answers in empirical work, but that all will have an opportunity to reflect on the sad but inevitable losses which they will encounter throughout life.

Loss in society

Human acts nearly always make sense. They arise from some
compromise between private impulse and social expectation.

(Barnlund 1976: 722)

In this first chapter, the concepts of bereavement, grief and mourning are
introduced and explored from cultural and historical perspectives, and the
interface between the subjective experience of loss and socio-cultural constraints will be considered.

Defining the key concepts

The *Oxford English Dictionary* (second edition, 1989) demonstrates the common root of the words bereavement and grief (reave), which is derived
from the Old English word 'reafian', to plunder, spoil or rob, and which
gave name to the reavers or reivers, bands of murdering brigands who
terrorized the debatable lands between the English and Scottish borders
before the Act of Union. Thus the root of the words denotes sudden,
forceful deprivation. Further, the loss is characteristically of 'some object
accustomed to draw forth the soothing or cheering reactions of the soul'
(Barnlund 1976: 722). These two aspects of loss by death – the sense of
personal violation and the heaviness of the soul – are thus embedded in
the language itself.

Scholars of various persuasions have made reference to death since scholar-
ship began, but it is generally agreed that the clinical study of reactions to
loss began in the early years of the twentieth century with Freud's (1917)
Mourning and Melancholia, in which he subsumes the behavioural and emotional changes set in train after a significant death under the single term
'mourning'. Bowlby (1960) also used the term; at first in a broader sense,
to cover the wide variety of reactions to loss, whatever their outcome, and
later to argue that there is a difference between grief and mourning, and to
describe mourning as 'the public act of expressing grief . . . always in some
degree culturally determined . . . distinguishable, at least conceptually, from

an individual's spontaneous responses' (p. 17). Averill (1968) also makes this distinction; for him, mourning is the conventional behaviour, determined by the mores and customs of the society, whereas grief is a set of stereotyped responses, psychological and physiological, of biological origin. He acknowledges, however, that both grief and mourning are subject to considerable variation, depending on the history and circumstances of the bereaved. In contemporary thinking, the distinction continues to be made. Stroebe *et al.* (1993a: 5) have given brief definitions of the key concepts: *bereavement*, the loss of a significant other person in one's life, which typically triggers a reaction we call *grief*, which is manifest in a set of behaviours we call *mourning*.

Grief has been defined in terms of mental pain, distress and deep or violent sorrow: bitter feelings of regret for something lost. Mourning, on the other hand, has two aspects: one subjective and rooted in anxiety, pining, remembrance, dying and withering, and the other in the public expression of grief and the exhibiting of conventional or ceremonial signs of grief such as the wearing of appropriate garments.

Many writers, then, have suggested that while loss and grief are universal in humans and are also shared with certain other species, mourning is culturally determined. However, there is controversy about how separable the concepts of grief and mourning are, and about the appropriateness of the attribution of grief to other species, as will be explored in this chapter.

How universal is grief?

Bereavement is universal in humankind, and it has been argued that other sentient species share some aspects of and reactions to it. Grief, the 'primarily emotional reaction' to such loss, 'which incorporates diverse psychological and physical symptoms' (Stroebe and Schut 1998: 7), has been observed across human cultures and throughout recorded human history, and is also considered by some writers to be manifest in other species as diverse as geese, dogs, elephants and non-human primates. We cannot know with certainty whether the calling and searching observed and described so poignantly by Konrad Lorenz (1966) in a greylag goose which had lost its mate, or the agitation and restlessness followed by a reduction in motor and feeding behaviour in response to a lost mother or mate in non-human primates, is merely a fixed action pattern, or the outward expression of an internal state we would recognize as grief. Studies have demonstrated the presence of physiological markers of 'distress' in separated animals – for example, raised pituitary/adrenal function in baby squirrel monkeys, and behavioural indicators of disturbance such as characteristic cries in the initial phase, and reduced adrenocortical output subsequently, when behaviour was also reduced (see, for example, Archer 1990; Laudenslager *et al.* 1993). In species such as elephants and apes, carrying or repeated returning to a dead offspring, holding and stroking, seen in mothers, appears like human grief, although we have no way of knowing directly about the inner state it represents. It is regarded by many people as so closely resembling human behaviour in similar situations that it is believed to correspond to our own experiences. Indeed, Harlow *et al.* (1972: 714), in describing the behavioural reactions of infant monkeys to separation, draw parallels with childhood depression and go so far as to argue that 'no thinking man has, and no thinking man ever will, question an enormous, near total generality from man'. However, humankind is, as far as we can tell, distinguished from other species by the capacity to apprehend not only a future, but a future in which death, including that of the self, is inevitable and irreversible, and this alone may suggest that human grief is qualitatively and fundamentally different from that shown by other animals. Further, attractive as the arguments for universality may be, they are based on the notion of 'normal' and universal behaviours in response to loss which we cannot uphold with any certainty in our own species, and we may, therefore, be advised to be cautious in attributing them to others, as will be discussed later in this chapter.

Bowlby (1980) has argued that the behaviours seen in humans in response to the death of a loved one represent a reaction to the loss of an attachment figure, and as such are of survival value. The restless searching and calling are attempts to find the crucial lost one, and when those attempts are unsuccessful, despair, characterized by apathy and withdrawal, ensues. Bowlby characterizes this transition in his description of an infant separated from his mother: 'His initial response . . . is one of protest and of urgent effort to recover his lost mother . . . Sooner or later, however, despair sets in. The longing for mother's return does not diminish, but the hope of it being realised fades' (p. 9); and in his description of a widow's 'restlessness, insomnia, preoccupation with thoughts of the lost husband combined with a sense of his actual presence, and a marked tendency to interpret signals or sounds as indicating that he is now returned' (p. 9). Parkes (1996) also comments on the awareness of a need to search for the lost one, the adoption of a general perceptual set that scans sensory input for evidence of the missing person, and the sense of being drawn to places or objects associated with them, or to the hospital where they died.

It may be argued, however that in many cases, bereavement does not threaten the survival of those left behind in the same way that the loss of a mother figure threatens an infant. Averill's (1968) view of grief is that the threat and unpleasantness associated with separation has an evolutionary advantage; it is to prevent separation and promote group cohesion in species capable of individual recognition and attachment. In such species, the chances of survival for individuals are enhanced by staying with the group. Marris (1992) takes a more specifically human perspective in arguing that grief is provoked not merely by the loss of a significant relationship itself but by 'the disintegration of the whole structure of meaning centred upon it' (p. 18), and that it is the enormity of this threat that provokes the anxiety, restlessness and distress. Thus both real and symbolic aspects of the loved one are grieved over, and the losses are manifest in private feelings and in public behaviour – death affects the wider community as well as those most closely concerned. Again, it may be argued that these are uniquely human features of bereavement, but at what point in our evolution did they develop?

The history of grief

Although a sense of loss and therefore grief may, for all we know, date back at least to the time when the first anthropoids were recognizable as human, it is only in relatively recent years and in some societies that entire industries have grown up around death and its aftermath. Many old myths contain the idea of a golden age before death existed, and suggest that it was called into being by some mischief or mistake, or to keep humankind from challenging the gods. Ancient stories and legends also speak of the struggle humankind has long been engaged in to come to terms with the finality of death and to deal with its aftermath in individuals and societies. Early writings tell us that bereavement has been known as a source of physical and mental disturbance in those left to mourn, since stories began. In one of the earliest known poems in the English language, 'The Wanderer', circa AD 850 (Etchells 1988: 31), the poet mourns 'Here possessions are fleeting, here friends are fleeting, here man is fleeting, here kinsman is fleeting, the whole world becomes a wilderness', and in the early Greek myths, when the goddess Demeter loses her daughter Persephone she loses 'her gaiety for ever' (Graves 1955: 89). Demeter shows the characteristic restlessness and emotional turmoil of acute grief: she seeks her child for nine days and nights without rest, food or drink, and when she hears that Hades (death) has taken her, she is so angry that she is ready to destroy everything living on Earth. The desolation, restlessness and raging against death shown in these early accounts are familiar to us today. Now, almost at the end of the twentieth century, the methods of enquiry and foci of interest may be new, but the struggle to make sense of death goes on essentially unchanged. What do we know about the origins of that struggle?

In the absence of written records, our knowledge of the behaviour of our early ancestors is necessarily patchy and speculative, based as it is on the placing and types of ancient fragments, natural and manufactured, of their lives. We know that, at some point in the long distant past, probably between 50,000 and 80,000 years ago, human remains began to be buried or disposed of in a deliberate and sometimes ritualistic way. The exact timing of the transition is in dispute (see, for example, Chase and Dibble 1987). Wymer (1982: 164–5) has described the adoption of these practices as marking the transition from savagery to barbarism, and has commented that they coincide with archaeological evidence of significant changes in the economy of hunting groups. The evidence suggests that humans had evolved to the point of trying to comprehend and thus control certain aspects of their environment – perhaps 'to grasp the notion of a future' (Feifel 1998: 3).

The change from simply leaving a corpse for the natural processes of decay and predators to deal with, to undertaking the group effort of burial, is considerable. At the very least it indicates a concern with things other than immediate survival; burial is no longer a simple matter of hygiene, it has become a symbolic act. There is no basic biological reason to expend time and energy, that might have been devoted to the acquisition of food, to the burial of the dead. It can thus be regarded as a social act also, of significant value for the group. It must also have involved cooperation, and therefore in some sense, discussion. It appears to have been selective; not everyone was accorded burial. Grave goods have been found in some graves, and although it has been argued that on some sites the placement was accidental, there are instances of flint knives placed in the hands of corpses. Other evidence of symbolism includes red ochre having been strewn on the corpse, placement on a bed of seashells, in one instance a 'crown' of goats' horns around the head and in another a bear's skull in the corpse's arms. We cannot know the precise intentions of those who buried their dead in such a way, but we may deduce that they continued to care for that member of their group even after death, as they protected the body. They also kept the bodies close by; intentional burials are associated with dwelling sites, unpleasant though that must have been when the natural processes of decay took hold, and although as Wymer (1982: 250) has pointed out, 'the reason . . . is contained in the now unfathomable thoughts of these people', it is the suggestion of *care* of the body and the implication of *thinking about* its disposal which are important. The evidence gleaned from these early burials may be taken to imply the capacity to imagine; to have a sense of an 'other' which cannot be seen or experienced directly, and to have a sense of the future. Somewhere in our early history we developed the capacity for symbolic thought, and alongside it the notion of a journey associated with death; of something leaving the body when it died and continuing to exist in another form, elsewhere.

As larger social groups accrued, with the development of an agrarian economy and the increasing manufacture and use of tools, the ritualistic disposal of the dead continued to be selective and became more elaborate. There are intimations of religious practices. Grave mounds were sometimes aligned to the east (to the rising sun), and sacrifices appear to have been made on or near some grave sites. Thus it appears that from our earliest days there have been rituals concerned with death which were important enough to involve the community, or some members of it, in hard physical work, which often imply continuation elsewhere – the notion of a spirit or soul released from the body to journey on – and which also give strong social status messages.

These two aspects of funeral rites – messages about the stability of the ongoing group and its structures, and messages about the change death has brought to the individual member, who is now 'elsewhere', are universal. They are expressed in many different ways across cultures and throughout history, and a variety of religious beliefs are associated with them and the fate of the soul. Pharaonic burials in ancient Egypt became so elaborate that they were of necessity planned many years in advance. The pyramids were unimaginably costly in terms of goods, working hours and the lives of workers, who seem not to have been accorded any kind of rituals to send *their* souls on their onward journeys. The bodies of those high in social standing were preserved by mummification and buried with costly grave goods. Nobody knows what happened to the bodies of the ordinary citizens, the poor, or the slaves. In early China, members of the household of a high-ranking person were sometimes slaughtered on his or her death and buried in a huge grave with their lord or lady. These historical facts tell us nothing directly about personal grief, they only reveal its public face, but they indicate the importance accorded to the 'right' treatment of (at least some) dead bodies.

As societies spread and diversified, so did the rituals. Across the world today, the 'right' way to deal with death and its aftermath is almost unimaginably variable. In some cultures the total obliteration of every trace of the physical body is crucial to the future well-being of the soul, as in Hinduism, and in others the preservation of the body by embalming is equally significant. In some cultures, such as the Yolngu of Australia (Eisenbruch 1984a: 339–40) the dead body is considered to be a source of dangerous pollution and everyone associated with it is unclean and must undergo ritual cleansing. In others, such as the Berawan of northern Borneo, the body is cared for lovingly (Huntington and Metcalf 1979).

Religious beliefs associated with death may give comfort to the living if they contain messages of eternal rest, heaven or rebirth, or may be used to control behaviour if they threaten punishment after death for misdeeds committed during life. Thus the neglect of appropriate rites may cause mere uneasiness or social censure in more 'sophisticated' societies, whereas in others it will blight the family for generations and require repeated and often costly propitiatory ceremonies. It is customary, for example, for family members to 'follow' the corpse in most English subcultures, and great embarrassment and distress was caused in one family in a rural area when the funeral of a distant relative was not known about. Not only were they not able to follow the hearse, but there were no other followers, which was considered to be disrespectful to the deceased and a disgrace for the family. They felt obliged to explain to their neighbours that their apparently lax behaviour was because of a mistake, and was not a deliberate slight to the deceased, but that was, essentially, the end of the matter. The consequences of the neglect of appropriate rites were far more serious in Firth's (1993) account of a doctor's refusal to let the family put Ganges water into the mouth of a dying Gujerati woman ('because the shock might kill her'). The family's belief was that, as a result, the soul of the woman would be restless, and require propitiation at family events such as marriages, for seven generations. The great difficulties experienced when people from one culture, with strong traditions about death and dying, migrate to another culture where the traditions are different, are well described by Eisenbruch (1984b).

Purposes served by funeral rites

The meaning and importance of funeral rites is beyond question, but their public nature and their usage at emotionally-charged occasions may lead them to be used as vehicles for a variety of messages which have nothing to do with grief.

It is evident from the elaborate, costly and time-and-effort-consuming nature of funeral rites in many cultures that they serve important social purposes. We must function within our social group, and by meeting its expectations we identify ourselves to some extent, but such expectations can also inhibit the expression of individual needs if they are applied too rigidly and in the absence of good social support. Averill (1968: 727) comments: 'death rites are a complex blend of customs fashioned to meet the needs of society as well as those of the individual bereaved. Where these needs are in conflict, social prerequisites typically precedent over the desires and well-being of the individual'. However, there are also many examples in history and across cultures where funeral and mourning rites exclude some members of the group; in some religious/cultural groups, for example Hindus, the souls of children are not considered to be developed before a certain age, and they are not accorded rites. Here in Britain some churches have only recently developed rites for miscarried and stillborn babies (Grainger 1998: 117). A further example was the old tradition of refusing to allow people who died by suicide to be buried in consecrated land.

Ritual burials are also practised for companion animals by increasing numbers of people, although some writers have argued that the loss of a beloved pet is an occasion for sorrow but not grief except in some particular circumstances (McNicholas and Collis 1995). In all these examples, the worth of the lost one to society may be painfully at odds with the worth to individuals.

There are also examples of public rites being hijacked to serve the ends of powerful groups rather than the mourners. Littlewood (1992: 30) comments on situations in which some bereaved people accrue significant disadvantage by the constraints of societal prescriptions about mourning. However, some of these prescriptions contain distinct commercial advantages for some sections of society. For example, the seventeenth-century Acts for Burying in Woollen were an attempt to lessen the need for imported goods, and to encourage the wool manufacturers by levying a fine of £5 if linen shrouds were used (Litten 1997: 48). Later, the importance and expense of 'correct' mourning dress in the nineteenth century for those on low incomes often meant an uncomfortable choice between the shame and anguish of failing to show appropriate behaviour towards the deceased, and increased penury in order to meet the expenses.

Other examples of rituals and practices which have been, and are, usurped by powerful groups or the establishment include those which frighten and subdue ordinary people, such as those associated with terrorist funerals in Northern Ireland in which masked and armed men accompanied the cortège and fired volleys of shots over the grave, and the threatening and 'magical' elements of the Haitian zombie cult. These abuses are not new; history provides us with a sorry catalogue of other examples.

The public mutilation of the corpses of 'criminals' (such as hanging, drawing and quartering; beheading and displaying the head on a pike; burying the body in quicklime) not only acted as a grim lesson for the living, but contained the suggestion of punishment continuing even after death. Such punishment is also enshrined in The Anatomy Act of 1832, which allowed the bodies of paupers to be used for dissection in medical schools, when the increase in demand meant that the supply of murderers' cadavers was insufficient. As Richardson (1988) points out, part of the punishment for murder was the mutilation of the body by dissection, and the Act transferred that grisly fate to the poor.

The pain for the bereaved must have been exacerbated beyond measure by these practices. The continuing sentience of the corpse, or the presence of the soul in the body, at least for a while after death, was and is a widespread belief and many rituals associated with the body are concerned with continuing the care of the soul (and sometimes encouraging it to leave the body and the realm of the living). Furthermore, some religious beliefs about resurrection require the body to be intact so that it can be reunited with the soul when the time comes. Thus, these punishments were, in effect, eternal.

In modern times, there remains considerable ambivalence about the use of body parts for organ transplantation following death, despite its recognition as a successful treatment for certain severe end-stage diseases, such as renal failure. This probably relates to long-established beliefs about the value of body integrity after death, and social distaste at bodily mutilation. In Britain, while the majority of the population approve of and accept the need for cadaveric organ transplantation, only about one third of people carry an organ donor card. Sque and Payne (1996) studied the bereaved relatives of the deceased organ donors, many of whom had died in road traffic accidents. The authors described the process by which the bereaved relatives decided whether to donate the body parts of their deceased loved ones. Even in this sample, who were sympathetic to organ donation, a group refused to donate certain organs, especially corneas, because of the symbolic significance of the eyes which were described by one participant as being 'a window to the soul'. Sque and Payne proposed a model of 'dissonant loss' to explain this unusual type of bereavement, where parts of the deceased continue to live on in the bodies of organ recipients. According to the participants this did not alter the feelings of loss and grief but it did help them to find meaning from an otherwise frequently shocking and sudden death.

The activities of punishment referred to previously had and have little or nothing to do with the grief of the ordinary people involved, but are a demonstration of the public, social aspects of bereavement being used in order to further other ends. In such cases, the public ritual of 'mourning' may not reflect the needs of the individuals most closely involved, and may leave them with disturbing messages about the meaningfulness of their loved one's life and the fate of their soul. It may be argued that where there is insufficient public acknowledgement of private griefs and concerns, it may be felt by mourners that their loved one or their own strong feelings are disregarded or diminished, and this in turn might make grief and adaptation to the loss problematic. What happens to people in a situation in which their feelings and needs are not recognized?

In many western societies, the assumption is that such lack of recognition may lead to 'abnormal' grieving, but caution must be exercised in extending our notions of normal and abnormal to other societies. There is evidence from the anthropological literature of the extent to which social mores shape individual responses. Wikan's (1989) well-known account of the 'bright face' of the Balinese is a particularly dramatic example of the social shaping of grief. In Bali, the expression of emotions is a matter of great concern for the group, and is the subject of stringent sanctions. Freeflowing emotions, particularly negative ones like grief and anger, are considered dangerous – 'angry hearts' are responsible for misfortune and bad health. Moreover, these negative emotions are contagious, so one person's grief may threaten the whole group. Thus managing the heart by keeping a bright face is the ideal, and is practised energetically. Wikan tells of a tragically bereaved young woman apparently being almost bullied into laughing soon after her fiancé was killed ('This is nothing to be sad about! The world is full of men! No use grieving over one! Go on, be happy!' (Wikan 1989: 297)). If she was quiet and thoughtful, she complained that someone would leap at her and tell her to stop it: 'You make us unhappy by that withered face. Now stop it! Be happy! Make your heart better!' (p. 297). A year later, Wikan reminded the girl that she had been angry with the others because of their laughter, and the girl defended them: 'Oh no! They laughed to take the sadness out! They laughed to make my heart happy from sadness' (p. 297).

From a western perspective, this is an example of prescribed behaviour which would be regarded as abnormal and likely to lead to psychological disturbance later, and yet this does not appear to be the case. Wikan describes the 'well-tested' ethnotheory of emotion, in which inner feelings are shaped by their outward expression, and spread easily to others. This is akin to Bates' (1987) biocultural model which addresses the relationship between overt acts and social appropriateness, and private experiences. Bates uses pain as her model of biocultural shaping of experience and behaviour, but it could as well apply to other states of being. Her thesis is that social and cultural learning shape not only outward behaviour but habitual cognitive responses and physiological reactions – for example, learned values and attitudes affect attention to painful stimuli and memory of pain experiences. It is easy to see how this model could be applied to bereavement, and make the link between grief and mourning. It would account for the variety of expressions of grief in the world, and the fact that different though they are, most of them do not give rise to abnormality if they keep the balance between individual and societal needs.

There are, of course, occasions when a mismatch between individual needs and public requirements does cause problems for individuals. Lewis (1966) argues that the stipulated prolonged mourning of Victorian times 'made the dead far more dead' (p. 48), and that it prevented reconnection with the deceased: 'the less I mourn her the nearer I seem to her' (p. 48), is how he described his own journey through grief after the death of his wife. Some writers have argued that we have seen another such mismatch, in the opposite direction, in this country since the First World War. At the outset of the war, the full mourning dress and elaborate rules for behaviour of those closest to the deceased were still current, but the scale of the slaughter was such that the whole country (especially women) would have been plunged into black, and it was discouraged (Taylor 1983). After the war, the habit of subdued mourning remained, and collective national ritual was instituted with the eleventh hour of the eleventh day of the eleventh month being annually devoted to national remembrance of those who died in that and subsequent wars.

Marris (1958) drew attention to the lack of comfort in the low-key funeral practices which characterized post-war Britain, but in what way was it different from the emotional control witnessed by Wikan in Bali, which did not cause obvious long-term problems? There are two elements to consider: first, the low-key practices were new, and had developed in a very short space of time to meet a need born of trauma; they had not evolved with the group's longer-term needs. Second, although in Bali negative emotions are proscribed, people are not left to mourn alone and unsupported. Other people show great interest in them and their plight, and it may be that the crucial element in this is the attention they show to the bereaved, particularly as its intention is to be helpful.

In recent years, the inadequacies of the modern funeral and expected mourning behaviour commented on by Marris (1992) have become a wider and more public cause of concern. Walter wrote a book called *Funerals and How to Improve Them* in 1990, and has recently expanded on his concerns about the inhibition of grief in England, where a complex set of social norms acts so as to discourage not only the public expression of grief but also its expression in formal rituals (Walter 1997a). However, Walter sees signs of change latterly, and argues that a new norm of expressive grief is becoming established. Grainger (1998) reports on the establishment of The National Funerals College, set up in 1995 with a mandate to give a better service to the bereaved. The college has produced *The Dead Citizen's Charter* (Johnson 1996) in which concern is expressed about the lack of attention to the needs of mourners – for things such as adequate time, meaningful symbolism, and an appropriate appreciation of the life of the deceased. The Charter draws attention to the fact that funeral rites can serve the wider society and the individual alike, and that the living and the dead should both be served by those rites.

Grainger (1998) argues that effective funeral rites contain the tripartite elements of the rites of passage described by Van Gennep (1995). Rites of passage have a threefold function: separation (dismissal), transition (chaos) and reintegration (incorporation). Their importance in societies is in maintaining systems which must outlive their individual members by marking the transitions from one state to another throughout life with unchanging public rituals. Societies all over the world use rituals to mark events such as the transition from childhood to adulthood (for example, the Jewish bar mitzvah, the Fijian first menstruation celebration), from the single to the married state, and from life to death. Van Gennep argued that they all contained the same three elements through which the person is separated from their old social status, undergoes a period of transition during which they may be isolated from the group, and is then reincorporated into their new state. So, in a funeral rite the dead person will be separated from the living (e.g. put in a coffin), will be sent away, and will then be reincorporated (for example, in memories, in memorial rites, by becoming an ancestor).

Littlewood (1992) argues that the rites offer not only a way of dealing with the disturbance caused by death, but a structure which can also assist understanding of the newly bereaved – they too often undergo a period of isolation while they deal with the death, and must then undergo the transition back to the world of the living and take on a new status, such as that of a widow. While the main purpose of these rites is to serve the society, the individual will also benefit by taking part in a shared experience and thus having group ties and structures reinforced, by having their grief legitimized by the group, and by being provided with 'an articulated scenario of the process of mourning and an opportunity to act out the various components or stages of emotional distress involved in the grief reaction' (Grainger 1998: 110). At a deeper and more personal level, the messages of the rite also become internalized. Pegg and Metze's (1981) book *Death and Dying: A Quality of Life* contains an account by Astrid Andersson Wretmark which demonstrates the significance of this process. As a hospital chaplain she conducts funerals for stillborn babies, and is sometimes alone in the chapel when she does so. She writes that she conducts the rites to show respect 'to the least of His brethren, and by doing so to show respect for life itself' (Pegg and Metze 1981: 64). Even when there is no one to share in the rite or witness it, it still has a powerful personal meaning for her. In Wretmark's case, this is clearly bound up in her particular faith, but affiliation to a recognized religious faith is not a prerequisite for depth of meaning in the performance of a funeral rite; it is a reflection of an internalized set of values and beliefs.

Firth (1961: 63–5) identifies other functions of funerals, through which both private and public concerns may be met via appropriate and sensitive rituals:

1 they help bereaved people to deal with their uncertainty by marking the end of the life in a distinctive, well-recognized way;
2 they allow the other members of the community to make public recognition of the loss, say goodbye, and express 'the powerful emotions of anger and fear that are often engendered' by death;
3 they are an occasion for the exchange of goods and services by which each may lay claim to assistance from the others in the future.

Hubert (1992: 11) also suggests a number of reasons why reverence and ritual in the disposal of remains was, and continues to be, important for the other members of the family or group of the deceased:

1 they may reflect concern for the wishes and feelings expressed by the person while they lived. This is an important message for those left behind – that the dead will not be discarded as soon as they die, and will have continuing respect and importance in the lives of those who loved them. As Annwn (1997) wrote in his poem 'Journey': 'and now I know that, like the moon hidden at mid-day, I will never pass away but only pass into the heart of all things'.
2 The remains themselves may be respected as revered ancestors or 'known and beloved kin recently dead'. That the care accorded to people while they lived goes on is also a reassuring message for the bereaved.
3 There may be respect for the spirits of the dead that they may rest in peace, or that an unquiet or potentially malevolent spirit should be appeased. An example of this is the belief common to many Native American tribes that unless the body is buried in the earth, its spirit is doomed to wander in limbo for eternity.

The nub of these rites is the acknowledgement of an ongoing but changed relationship with the deceased. It may be argued that successful mourning rituals mark that change, sometimes in a dramatic fashion, both for the individuals most closely concerned with the deceased, and for the larger group. To return to Van Gennep's (1965) theory, we might add to Hubert's (1992) list the need to confront the chaos and unthinkableness of death by long-established and well-known formal behaviour patterns (rituals), which restate group identity and contain the individual mourners while they are emotionally volatile and vulnerable. By prescribing not only mourning but grief itself, societies seek to maintain their own cohesion, contain the upset of the individual members and draw paths back to 'normality' – that is, appropriate social functioning. 'Pathology' is described in terms of inappropriate functioning/dysfunction for that society, and as we in the West have latterly sought to understand dying, death and grief in medical and professional terms, we invoke theories such as 'grief work' (Freud 1917; Worden 1991), 'phases' (Bowlby 1980; Parkes 1996), the 'Dual Process Model' (DPM) (Stroebe and Schut 1996) which will be described in detail in later chapters.

Many books on bereavement include a personal account to illustrate the process of grief and mourning to the reader and give them some insight into the experience. We have decided not to do this, but instead suggest that readers turn to Young and Cullen's (1996) moving account of the dying, deaths and bereavement of a small sample of East Londoners. Their book, *A Good Death*, vividly illustrates the process of loss, set in the context of cockney culture, in the latter part of the twentieth century.

Conclusion

It can be argued that there is a large degree of social determination of grief as well as mourning – they are not easy to separate – and that the function of grief is to adjust to the loss so that society and the individuals in it can go on functioning in spite of the change the loss has caused. In some cases this will involve efforts to return to the status quo before the loss, and in others it will involve efforts to incorporate a permanent change in some aspects of life.

Inevitably there are sometimes tensions between the needs of the individual and the society. Some societies attempt to deal with these tensions by eliminating the deceased or minimizing their impact, but it is more usual to acknowledge that the loss was significant – even if only to a few people – and thus to sanction the disruption to life and the effort required to reorganize and go on. This can be highly ritualized, and in our society is medicalized and professionalized; our rituals are concerned with phase theory, grief work, bereavement counselling and so on, and these concepts and activities are no different in essence from those practised by other societies. Instant remarriage of the widow at the graveside and 'bright face' both serve societies' need to regain and maintain normality, and therefore the needs of their individual members, in a way that makes sense in terms of their history and cultural identity.

Ideally, then, mourning rituals and expectations about 'right' grief behaviour should serve the group by enabling the individual. Where there is a good match between individual needs and group provision, the 'chaos' of loss should be contained for all. If, however, the group neither provides adequate acknowledgement of the life of the deceased nor of the needs of the bereaved, or it develops 'stories' which neither provide group support nor correspond to what people need or feel, perhaps 'abnormal' grief is more likely as people struggle with the dissonance between their own needs and feelings and the message from the group. As it is, we now have evidence of the development of personal rites in some countries, arising from groups of people with particular unmet needs. Grainger (1998) writes of a new Catholic liturgy for stillborn and miscarried children, and the Cumbrian theatre company Welfare State, which specializes in constructing rites of passage is including funerals in its repertoire. Klass and Heath (1996) have written about the Japanese 'children of the water' rites for aborted babies, a modern variant of the traditional ancestor worship, which has arisen to fill the need to acknowledge the grief after abortion (now the most common form of birth control in Japan, and usually performed after the family has reached its preferred size). The rite not only acknowledges the grief of the parents, it maintains a connection between the living parents and the dead child, so that the 'bitterness, ill will, enmity, spite or malice' the dead child might feel because it is alone and neglected will be prevented (Smith 1974: 44). The rite has grown out of, and is a variation on, ancient and deeply held beliefs and traditions in which remaining connected to one's ancestors is of central importance.

Studies such as those by Klass and Heath (1996) and Wikan (1989) provide compelling evidence of alternative, culture-specific patterns of behaviour in response to loss, and Grainger's (1998) account of the development of new rites shows how these may evolve in response to the needs of individuals. We must make sense of catastrophic events like bereavement with reference to cultural norms and expectations; a culture's death and mourning customs are an expression of its core values regarding the nature of the individual and of life (Huntington and Metcalf 1979). Thus 'bright face' as a way of dealing with loss is no more and no less valid a model than phase theory, in that they both serve the function of guiding the individual in their behaviour and allowing a return to normal functioning after the loss has been accommodated, at both group and individual levels.

Summary

◆ Grief may be said to be universal in humans – and perhaps other species – in the sense that it is a set of responses to significant loss, which provokes the need to adapt.
◆ The biological and societal aspects of reaction to loss have been differentiated as *grief* and *mourning* by some writers, but it may be argued that both have a large socially-shaped component – see Wikan's (1989) ethnotherapy of emotion.
◆ Death has been imbued with symbolic meanings since prehistoric times. The way these meanings are expressed reflects the needs of the group

and the bereaved individuals to contain the disturbance caused by the death and reestablish a new order. Funeral rites characteristically promote group cohesion.

◆ Individual grief is facilitated when custom permits close attention to and support of the bereaved. The form the attention and support takes is highly culturally specific.

Further reading

Eisenbruch, M. (1984a) Cross-cultural aspects of bereavement. I: A conceptual framework for comparative analysis. *Culture, Medicine and Psychiatry*, 8: 283–309.

Eisenbruch, M. (1984b) Cross-cultural aspects of bereavement. II: Ethnic and cultural variations in the development of bereavement practices. *Culture, Medicine and Psychiatry*, 8: 315–47.

Field, D., Hockey, J. and Small, N. (eds) (1997) *Death, Gender and Ethnicity*. London: Routledge.

Frazer, J. (1993) *The Golden Bough*. Ware: Wordsworth Reference.

Grainger, R. (1998) *The Social Symbolism of Grief and Mourning*. London: Jessica Kinglsey Publications.

Huntington, R. and Metcalf, P. (1979) *Celebrations of Death: The Anthropology of Mortuary Ritual*. Cambridge: Cambridge University Press.

Parkes, C.M., Laungani, P. and Young, B. (eds) (1997) *Death and Bereavement Across Cultures*. London: Routledge.

Young, M. and Cullen, L. (1996) *A Good Death*. London: Routledge.

The impact of loss: stress and coping

While the last chapter introduced the terms bereavement, grief and mourning, and considered them against the backdrop of cultural, social and historical changes, this chapter focuses upon the individual response to loss. It examines the burden of grief borne by individuals, the expression of grief and its impact on health. Even though patterns of response are mediated by cultural and social factors, individuals display reactions to loss in very different ways. This chapter describes responses in terms of physiological, cognitive/emotional, behavioural, sexual and spiritual changes. Clearly these are not discrete categories, in that emotional expression, such as crying, affects physiological functions such as breathing patterns, but for easy of presentation, they will be discussed separately.

The next section considers the epidemiological evidence of health consequences, mortality and morbidity, due to bereavement and other major losses. The question 'Is it possible to die of a broken heart?' will be addressed, as well as the question as to whether major stressors precipitate or potentiate other long-term illnesses.

This approach to understanding the effects of loss and bereavement on individuals can be conceptualized as deriving from theoretical models of stress and coping. Therefore the final part of this chapter reviews two alternative theoretical positions. First, there is the notion that bereavement and loss function as stressors to which individuals are required to adapt. We draw on the early work of Holmes and Rahe (1967) in which loss, especially spousal bereavement, was classified as the most extreme stressor faced by an individual. Their approach, in which events were given relative scores and were conceived of as external stressors, is reviewed and critiqued. Second, more recent theoretical models, especially that described by Lazarus and Folkman (1984), have proposed that individual appraisals are the key determinant of perceived stress. We review the applicability of this approach to bereavement and loss, and briefly consider some of the mediating variables which may influence the perception of loss and the expression of loss, such as personality traits like hardiness (Kobasa 1979). We propose that there are individual differences in vulnerability and resilience which influence the impact of loss on health outcomes.

Individual responses to loss

We would argue that grief is not an illness or medical syndrome. It is a widely variable response which changes over time, probably not in a linear fashion, although this will be debated later in the book. Grief hurts. People describe feeling torn apart or as if they have lost part of themselves. It is often described as physically and emotionally painful. According to Bowlby (1980: 7), 'Loss of a loved person is one of the most intensely painful experiences any human being can suffer'. It is debatable whether there is a universal human *response* to loss (Wortman and Silver 1989). The anthropological evidence shows that physical and psychological expressions vary and that there are no universal *expressions* of loss (Parkes *et al.* 1997). Therefore the following should be read not as a definitive list but as an indication of the types of expressions of grief that may be encountered. In addition, readers should note that physical and psychological responses associated with grief are culturally bound and this book is written from a western (European and North American) perspective. Other responses not described here may be considered 'normal' in different cultures (Rosenblatt 1997), but there is limited research evidence from other cultures. The patterns of responses refer to adults, unless specifically stated. A description of the nature of the responses is presented before discussing the physiological and psychological mechanisms thought to account for them.

Physical responses

People may experience an alarming array of physical problems in the aftermath of a bereavement. Box 2.1 provides a brief list. Perhaps the commonest complaint is fatigue which may be described as loss of energy. Related to this people may experience loss of sleep or changes to their normal sleeping patterns as, for example, they adjust to the absence of a familiar partner to share their bed. Bereaved people experience a range of problems that are sometimes labelled 'psychosomatic' complaints. These include aches and pains resulting from muscular tension such as headaches, dizziness, neck stiffness and back pain. In addition, there may be changes to eating patterns with appetite suppression or overeating, such as 'comfort eating' of sweet foods like biscuits and chocolate. Other gastro-intestinal changes may occur such as nausea, vomiting, feelings of choking, perceptions of a lump in the throat or abdominal fullness, constipation or diarrhoea. More worryingly for them, bereaved people may start to experience similar symptoms of

---

Box 2.1   Physical responses to loss and bereavement

- Fatigue
- Sleep pattern changes, usually insomnia
- 'Aches and pains' – these can be very variable such as headaches, back pain, muscular aches, tightness in chest or throat
- Appetite changes – usually anorexia with resultant loss of weight
- Gastro-intestinal changes – nausea, vomiting, indigestion, constipation, diarrhoea
- Vulnerability to infection – increased incidence of minor infections such as colds

---

illness to those of the deceased. Finally, bereaved people appear to experience increased vulnerability to infections and other diseases.

Psychological responses

There are many psychological responses to loss and bereavement. According to Rosenblatt (1997), there are no universal emotional consequences of a death and all expressions of emotion and the meaning ascribed to them are culturally defined. Perhaps the most readily acknowledged consequence of loss is psychological distress. In fact, its absence in western societies is regarded as pathological, although the culturally approved expression of distress is mediated by factors such as relationship to deceased, gender, social class and age (Walter 1996b; Field *et al.* 1997). Box 2.2 offers an indicative list of the range of psychological responses encountered after loss.

Perhaps the commonest emotion experienced is sadness and depression. It is important to differentiate between levels and duration of depression, from transient feelings of sadness experienced by virtually everyone, to sustained periods of sadness and low mood as people adjust to irrevocable loss, and severe profound persistent clinical depression in which people are unable to undertake normal everyday tasks and which may lead to such feelings of worthlessness that suicide is contemplated or attempted. Most psychiatric textbooks describe the differences to be expected between clinical depression and other states of sadness and despair. Bereaved people often describe their suffering in terms of depression, especially in relation to the sadness, sorrowing and despair for the future. The depression of loss is likely to be variable, with particular events or memories triggering painful waves of sadness, which although diminishing over time can still recur years later.

Anxiety may be experienced alongside depression or alone. Parkes (1996) has argued that anxiety is the most common response to bereavement.

Box 2.2 Psychological responses to loss and bereavement

1 *Emotional*
- Depression – sadness, loss of pleasure response, low mood, intense distress
- Anxiety – fearfulness, separation anxiety
- Hyper-vigilance – inability to relax
- Anger – may be expressed as hostility to friends, family, health care workers or God
- Guilt – feelings of self-blame for some aspect of the deceased's death or care during dying
- Loneliness – feeling of being alone even when with others

2 *Cognitive*
- Lack of concentration and attention – memory loss for specific events or general problems in recalling information or attending to new information
- Preoccupation – repetitive thoughts especially about the deceased, sometimes needing to talk constantly about certain events like a traumatic loss
- Helplessness/hopelessness – coping response which is characterized by pessimism about the future
- Feeling of distance/detachment – experienced as sense of unreality

3 *Behavioural*
- Irritability – expression of anger and hostility, suspiciousness, distrust
- Restlessness – inability to settle to specific tasks or feel relaxed
- Searching – pacing, looking for deceased
- Crying – tears, sighing
- Social withdrawal – remaining isolated, rejecting social groups and friendship

---

People are fearful about how they will cope with the present situation and in the future. The anxiety can be experienced as physical tension which is exhausting and gives rise to some of the muscular aches and pains referred to earlier. Loss and bereavement often have profound consequences for people's lives and many adjustments are required. In times of stress, change can be construed as anxiety-provoking as new skills have to be learnt such as handling finances, or driving a car. Anger, hostility and guilt are common emotions following loss, especially if the death is attributed to particular events or people. For example, a murder is likely to be associated with feelings of anger towards the perpetrator, while a suicide may leave survivors with feelings of guilt. Guilt may be conceptualized to be in-turned anger. Even in less extreme situations, bereaved people may be angry that the deceased has left them alone to cope with, for example, rearing young children or running a family business. It is common for people to be angry with the way a life-threatening diagnosis is presented, or with the way doctors, nurses and other carers deal with events at the time of traumatic deaths, such as following a road traffic accident. Anger may also be expressed more generally towards an 'unfair God', with unanswerable questions such as 'Why did it happen to me?' Depending upon when in the life cycle the death occurred, there may be anger about feeling cheated of a shared future, such as a long awaited and eagerly anticipated retirement together.

Bereavement may result in cognitive changes which, like emotional reactions, are unlikely to be stable but fluctuate in their intensity and disruptiveness. Initially after the loss there might be reduced emotional expression and heightened awareness, described by Parkes (1996) as 'numbness'. There may also be a sense of unreality and discontectedness from the world. Some people describe this as functioning on 'autopilot'. Later, bereaved people may experience disturbances in concentration and lack of motivation which makes it difficult to understand new information or engage in complex cognitive activities. In addition, some people experience repetitive thoughts although this should be differentiated from the 'flashbacks', nightmares and overload of distressing cognitions characterized by post-traumatic stress disorder (PTSD). There is evidence that experiencing the deceased by seeing or hearing the person is relatively common and should not be construed as abnormal (Conant 1996; Young and Cullen 1996). At one time such halluncinations were thought to be uncommon and indicative of pathology but there is now evidence that they may well be helpful.

Behavioural expressions of distress include agitation or restlessness with constant searching for the deceased, despite cognitive awareness of the loss. Feelings of anger and hostility may present themselves as irritability, physical or verbal attacks on others or objects, social withdrawal and self-mutilation. These behaviours may be socially sanctioned in some cultures, such as tearing hair or clothes to display distress and anguish. Crying is commonly sanctioned at funerals and following a loss, especially for women in western societies. Repetitive sighing or yawning may also be behavioural indicators of distress. Overwhelming feelings of isolation, even when surrounded by others, have been described as common.

Responses to sexuality

Many books do not acknowledge that there are likely to be changes in sexual responses near the time of, and following a death. In fact, there is little known about the 'normal' pattern of responses, except it is thought to encompass great diversity. Some cultural groups define 'appropriate' sexual behaviour for mourners and especially for widows which usually involves abstinence. Within British society, there are no constraints on sexual activity or remarriage after spousal bereavement but it is generally not socially acceptable if sexual activity or remarriage occurs 'too early', especially for women, which usually means within the first 6 to 12 months following the loss.

Writing from a clinical psychiatric perspective, MacElveen-Hoehn (1993) identified six sexual responses to the stimulus of death. She argued that the first involved complete withdrawal from sexual activity, with loss of libido, and impotence in men. The second response, she suggested, was typical of women who continued to engage in sexual behaviour with partners but lacked interest and desire. The third category was characterized by no change in usual sexual activity and no noticeable impact on desire. In the fourth category it was noted that people used sexual activity as a coping response to elicit comfort and solace. MacElveen-Hoehn argued that in this category people sought the comfort of being held, and the pleasure of bodily contact was the important element rather than the excitement of sexual arousal. The fifth category includes those people who find exposure to the stimulus of death a source of compelling desire for sexual activity. These people may seek new partners or try new sexual experiences in ways that may be untypical of their previous behaviour. MacElveen-Hoehn differentiates between this and the final category in terms of feeling states. In the fifth category, she suggests that sexual feelings become heightened but in the final category, people experience limited or no feelings associated with increased sexual activity. They report an absence of pleasure or a sense of detachment. MacElveen-Hoehn presents clinical case studies as evidence for the above categories of response. However, readers should be aware that there is limited research evidence for these claims as people who seek psychological support may not be representative of the general population. Moreover, it is not known how many people fall into the different categories.

It is perhaps safe to conclude that there is great diversity in sexual responses to the threat of loss and bereavement. As sexual activity may constitute one type of coping with loss, this can potentially present problems in partnerships where individuals react in different ways. For example, following the loss of a child, a woman may lose sexual desire and wish to be abstinent but her partner may cope by seeking the physical intimacy of sexual intercourse. It is clearly easy to see how rejection by the woman may be misconstrued by the partner, or vice versa. Yet diversity of sexual responses to death is rarely mentioned by health professionals, or others, providing support at such times. One reason may be that those providing support and counselling are aware of the risk that their behaviour may be misconstrued. For example, professionals and volunteers visiting bereaved people in their own homes need to ensure that their offers of support, especially if this involves physical touching or holding the person to comfort them, are not misconstrued as sexual advances or sexual availability.

Responses to spirituality

Loss and bereavement have traditionally been associated with spiritual aspects of humanity. Drawing on the work of King *et al.* (1994), it is proposed that it may be helpful to separate out three elements: religious, spiritual and philosophical beliefs. These aspects may not be present in all people – for example, some people profess to have no religious beliefs. It is also possible that two or more aspects may overlap – for example some people may have well-integrated religious, spiritual and philosophical beliefs. The diversity of individual responses noted in the previous sections holds true in relation to spirituality and religious belief, with some people finding solace within their meaning-making structure and others finding all previous beliefs destroyed. In some psychological accounts of coping (e.g. Carver *et al.* 1989) religious beliefs and practices are conceptualized as methods of coping. This will be dealt with in more depth later in the chapter.

Religion

Virtually all religions provide guidance and meaning for the experience of death, both for the dying person and for the bereaved. Religious beliefs represent one way in which people can structure their experience of life and death. They offer explanations which people may use to give meaning to death – for example, the concept of an afterlife. According to Walter (1997b) the deathbed rituals of Christianity, Hinduism and Islam are intended to ensure the safe passage of the soul from this world to the next. In the past this has justified the presence of the priest as an essential person attending the dying. Religions also guide behaviours around life transitions such as death and mourning rituals. Interested readers may review the following sources: Laungani (1997) describes a Hindu death and funeral in India and also (1996) presents an account of how traditional Hindu death rituals become modified by transition to another country (Britain).

In addition to specifying behaviours, religions may function as forms of community social support through factors such as providing companionship, practical help and supporting self-esteem via shared values and beliefs. In addition, being prayed for can provide comfort and increase self-worth. However, people may also feel let down and angry towards their religion or God, and a loss of faith may result if their church does not provide the anticipated help or support.

Research has typically emphasized measurable aspects of religious behaviour such as church attendance or belief in an afterlife. Less attention has been paid to the ways in which religions offer meaning to life events, especially when people are threatened by negative experiences. Walter (1997b) has discussed the role of religious beliefs in palliative care and offered a sociological analysis of trends in the secularization of hospices. Finally it may be important to recognize that people may vary in their degree of orthodoxy and no assumptions should be made that those who label themselves as 'belonging' to a specific religion will necessarily subscribe to all the beliefs and practices attributed to that group by others.

Focus on research

The role of Christian beliefs in coping with spousal bereavement in older English adults (Golsworthy and Coyle, in press)

A small qualitative study addressed the issue of how nine older people (mean age 67 years) used their existing Christian beliefs to find meaning following the loss of their spouse. Loss of a spouse is a severe challenge. Respondents were recruited via the minister at their local church and included people from the Church of England, the United Reformed Church, the Baptist Church and the Roman Catholic Church. They were interviewed by a clinical psychology trainee about the way their religion helped (or did not help) to give meaning to their experience of bereavement. Among the findings reported, people spoke of their faith and their personal relationship with God: 'Any time I got down or felt low, I just turned to the Lord and just prayed about it, I'd just talk it over with the Lord.'

The authors identified two groups of people: one who felt uncertain of their religious beliefs following the loss, and the other who remained confident in their beliefs but found that their beliefs did not give meaning to their continued existence without their partner. Only two people were easily able to find meaning in the death and a reason for their continued life. The majority of people did not think that their religious beliefs mitigated their feelings of grief but found relief in being able to help others, which is a strong Christian ethic.

Clearly this is a small study which may be biased by the recruitment of selected people by the ministers. There was insufficient diversity in the sample to be able to identify aspects of each religious group that were most or least helpful to bereaved people.

Spirituality

It has been argued that most people have spiritual beliefs even if they do not conform to specific religious doctrines (Stanworth 1997). In secular societies people may be more comfortable referring to their spiritual beliefs rather than to their religion. Individual understanding of spirituality may include existential issues that may be challenged by life crises such as bereavement. The experience of loss requires people to revise their assumptions of the world and their place within it (Barbato and Irwin 1992; Parkes 1996). Walter (1997b) has highlighted the dilemmas in health care contexts, especially palliative care, where religious ministry and care are seen to be the proper province of the chaplain but any member of staff can offer spiritual care and support outside of a religious framework. This suggests that only some people 'have' religion, which is a private matter, but that everyone has spiritual needs which should be assessed and attended to so that 'holistic' care can be accomplished. In contemporary Britain a wide range of spiritual beliefs may be encountered including New Age beliefs, paganism as well as the diversity of established religions. Consequently, people may have complex personal belief systems that cannot be neatly ascribed to one religious category.

Philosophical beliefs

Philosophical beliefs refer to broad approaches to life such as humanitarianism. They are generally taken for granted beliefs which are only raised to consciousness by ethical dilemmas or traumatic events such as suicide, multiple deaths or murder. The debate about the sanctity of life versus euthanasia is a good example for health professionals. Cultural groups may ascribe to differing philosophical values. Laungani (1996) highlights four philosophical dimensions which he argues characterize differing patterns of bereavement experience for Indian Hindus living in India, Indian Hindus living in Britain and white English people. They are: individualism versus communalism, cognitivism versus emotionalism, freewill versus determinism, and materialism versus spiritualism. These values are not regarded as dichotomous variables but as continuums on which people can be located. Individuals may have to compromise personal philosophical positions for the demands of the society in which they live. For example, Indian Hindus living in Britain are unlikely to be able to get 12 days off work following a bereavement to complete traditional mourning rituals. Thus it might be wrong to interpret more limited rituals as being indicative of a weakening attachment to religious beliefs in Indian Hindus living in Britain, because this may reflect situational constraints on behaviours imposed by British conventions: for example, 'normal' compassionate leave being just two or three days.

The effects of bereavement on health

What are the mechanisms which account for the health consequences of bereavement? Can people die of a broken heart? This section considers the epidemiological evidence on the mortality associated with bereavement. We will then discuss the possible mechanisms which account for increased mortality and morbidity following bereavement and other losses. These will include direct changes due to effects on immune and neuroendocrine functioning, and indirect effects which include both positive and negative lifestyle changes, alterations in health care behaviours, and social support.

Bereavement is a single event with multiple consequences so it is difficult, and perhaps inappropriate, to disentangle particular aspects.

There is a widespread commonsensical notion that people can be so traumatized by the loss of their loved one that it can change them forever (Queen Victoria is a good historical example), or can lead to their premature death – the so-called 'broken heart' syndrome. Among others, Stroebe and Stroebe (1987), Stroebe *et al.* (1993a) and Parkes (1996) provide good reviews of this topic. There appears to be strong evidence for a link between bereavement and increased mortality, especially in relation to spousal loss. Most research has focused on partners, although Parkes also cites evidence of increased mortality among parents following the loss of a child (Rees and Lutkins 1967) and even among grandparents (Roskin 1984). Stroebe (1993b) differentiates between cross-sectional surveys and longitudinal studies, both of which must be carefully controlled by matching bereaved people with those of a similar age, marital status and social class. It should be remembered that there is epidemiological evidence that married people experience health advantages compared to single (never married) people. There are additional high risk factors in post-bereavement mortality associated with the following variables which were reported by Stroebe (1993b):

♦ gender – mortality rates are higher in widowers than widows;
♦ age – younger compared to older widowers have greater mortality;
♦ social class – lower social classes have greater mortality which is in line with patterns for most diseases;
♦ duration of bereavement – there is a peak excess in mortality for widowers in the first six months, but a less clear pattern for widows;
♦ disease – there is evidence of increased deaths from heart disease, liver cirrhosis, suicide and other violent deaths, with less evidence for an increase in cancer deaths.

What physiological and psychological mechanisms account for increased post-bereavement mortality and morbidity?

There are likely to be a number of direct effects on physiology which may in themselves either cause disease or potentiate the effects of existing conditions. If bereavement is conceptualized as a stressor, it can be seen that the body will react to the increased arousal with the release of catecholamines such as adrenaline and noradrenaline. These initiate a cascade of neurophysiological changes associated with acute stress and over time, if the perception of threat remains dominant, chronic stress reactions occur. These reactions are described in more detail by Kim and Jacobs (1993). A meta-analysis of the literature on stress and immunity in humans indicates that, however stress is measured or manipulated, it is associated with a decrease in some aspects of immune system functioning (Herbert and Cohen 1993). Herbert and Cohen found that stress is also related to increases in white blood cells, immunoglobulin levels and antibody titres to herpes viruses.

Research has also demonstrated that bereavement and loss is associated with changes to immune function, especially immuno-suppression. Psychoneuroimmuniologists have shown an intimate but complex relationship between psychological perceptions of stress and immune function (e.g. Kiecolt-Glaser and Glaser 1986). It is possible that major stressors challenge immune functioning.

Focus on research

Ironson *et al.* (1997) followed up survivors of Hurricane Andrew at one and four months after the experience. They assessed people for symptoms of PTSD using a questionnaire and the Impact of Events scale (IES), and took blood for analysis. The results of the study showed that 33 per cent of the sample had PTSD, 76 per cent had at least one symptom cluster of PTSD and 44 per cent reported high impact on the IES. A major factor predicting a substantial proportion of the variance on PTSD was the experience of loss, damage, threat to life and injury. Raised white cell counts (a response to stress and infection) were significantly positively correlated with perception of loss and PTSD. Overall the sample had lowered levels of natural killer cell cytotoxicity, CD4 and CD8 numbers and higher NK cell numbers than laboratory controls. This study indicates that immune functioning changes in response to perceptions of loss.

Lindstrom (1997) examined coping, subjective perceptions of health and immunity following spousal bereavement in 39 Norwegian women. Data were collected 1 month and 13 months after the death. In this study changes in immunoglobin levels were not strongly related to subjective evaluations of health.

Reduced levels of immune function may make bereaved people susceptible to infections and could potentially make them vulnerable to developing cancer. In patients with already compromised immune function, such as those with HIV/AIDS, it is likely that multiple bereavements could precipitate a deterioration in their illness (Sherr 1995). The physiological consequences of stress such as increased blood viscosity and raised blood pressure may all be implicated in the mortality associated with coronary heart disease following bereavement but direct immunological changes are hard to separate out from effects of poor sleep, reduced appetite, self-neglect and other negative consequences of bereavement.

In addition, the consequences of bereavement may lead to a number of changes which result in indirect effects on health. We will focus on three possible causal mechanisms: lifestyle changes, health care behaviours and social support. As in the previous parts of this chapter, we wish to emphasize that these mechanisms should not be regarded as independent factors or necessarily applicable to all bereaved people. It is likely that while the majority of people cope well with life transitions, some experience problems either because of intrinsic vulnerabilities or because the cumulative burden over-taxes their resources. Change is not intrinsically harmful – in fact, without it people would not grow and develop psychosocially. The theoretical models of life transition and developmental approaches to bereavement will be dealt with more fully in the next chapter.

Lifestyle changes

Following a bereavement or other type of loss, people are likely to experience a number of lifestyle changes that may have an impact on their health. For example, elderly widows may experience a drop in income from lost pension entitlements which may mean that they cannot afford a 'healthy' diet high in fresh fruit and vegetables, cannot adequately heat their home in winter, cannot maintain regular repairs to their home or afford leisure activities. Elderly women, living alone, are among the most impoverished people in Britain. It is not difficult to envisage how these factors could lead to an increase in accidents such as falls in the home, hypothermia in winter and an increased susceptibility to infections.

Bereaved people may cope with their grief by using mood altering substances such as caffeine (for example, in coffee and chocolate), alcohol, nicotine, over-the-counter and prescription drugs. There are gender differences in the use of alcohol and nicotine but these are diminishing as consumption grows in women. Alcohol use may be implicated in the excess of deaths due to liver cirrhosis and in the high death rate from accidents. It could be that recently-bereaved people are vulnerable to accidents because they have trouble concentrating. It is possible that certain deaths categorized as accidents are in fact suicides due to dangerous and reckless driving.

Health care behaviours

Another important possible cause of increased mortality is changes in health care behaviours. These are likely to impact in a number of ways such as reduced motivation (or income) to eat appropriately. It is both more expensive and more difficult to buy smaller portions of food. Therefore, widows or widowers who live alone may change their diet to a 'less healthy' one. Research demonstrates that people often seek the views of others to interpret physiological stimuli which may indicate disease (Cacioppo *et al.* 1986). For example, early signs of myocardial infarctions (heart attacks) can be ambiguous and may be confused with indigestion. The presence of others makes it more likely that a person will be urged to seek health care and reduce the delay which, in the case of myocardial infarctions, can be critical to survival. The numerous symptoms associated with grief described earlier have many similarities with heart disease such as breathlessness, tightness in the chest and feeling faint. They are also similar to anxiety and therefore it is possible that people dismiss their symptoms and attribute them to grief. The reverse may also occur when people worry needlessly (which makes the anxiety worse) about dying and constantly seek medical care.

Social support

It is easy to see the important role social support plays in enhancing health behaviours such as encouraging early consultation, reducing some harmful behaviours and promoting maintenance of lifestyle changes such as changes to diet and smoking, as well as providing emotional support and enhancing self-worth. According to Carroll *et al.* (1993) there is consistent evidence from research concerning the interaction of health and social support to conclude that those with low levels of social support appear to experience increased mortality from a range of causes, increased morbidity, poorer prognoses and slower recovery. Bereavement changes the availability of social support, especially in spousal loss (Stroebe and Stroebe 1987).

However, it should be remembered that not all changes following bereavement are negative. If people are regarded as resilient and adaptive, most will experience positive as well as negative outcomes. For example, if they have been engaged in long-term care of the deceased such as in Alzheimer's disease, they no longer have those physical and emotional demands. In some cultures, the restrictions on the activities of a wife may be different to that of a widow, with more or less freedom to choose one's lifestyle. Disruptive, abusive and unsatisfactory relationships can be terminated by death which brings relief and offers opportunities to seek other more satisfactory relationships.

Theoretical models of stress

This chapter has been based on assumptions that bereavement and loss constitute major stressors. This section considers the theoretical models which seek to explain the impact of stress on health. We offer abbreviated accounts of the basic models as fuller accounts are available elsewhere, such as in the book *Stress* (Bartlett 1998) in this 'Health Psychology' series. The emphasis is on reviewing to what extent the models are helpful in explaining aspects of loss and bereavement.

It is common to attribute the introduction of the concept of stress to Hans Selye (1956), although Cannon (1932) first wrote about the 'fight or flight response' in the early part of this century. The classic 'fight or flight response' emphasized the physiological reaction to acute emergency situations, typically where people were in life-threatening contexts. Selye also emphasized the physiological component of stress in his formulation of the general adaptation syndrome, a three-phase response to stress. While these theories were important in describing physiological reactions, they took less account of the psychological concomitants of stress. They were also based on the assumption that different stressors produced similar responses which accounted poorly for individual differences.

An alternative approach to understanding stress is to focus on the stimuli which provoke the stress reaction. In this approach, there is no assumption that all stress responses are equally important. The first theory to emphasize psychological rather than physiological changes was developed by Holmes and Rahe (1967). They proposed that life changes (also called life events) were stressors that challenged the adaptational capacity of individuals, causing physical and psychological sequelae. Moreover these life events may be either positive or negative experiences. Holmes and Rahe proposed that the stress engendered by life changes results in reduced well-being and poorer health, and that the effects are cumulative, so that a greater number of life events requiring adaptation, whether positive or negative, would result in an increased probability of worse health.

Holmes and Rahe investigated their theory by developing the schedule of recent experiences (SRE), which is also known as the Social Readjustment Rating Scale (SRRS). They identified a list of 43 common events that might happen to people and ranked all the events, giving each event a score. The events were developed from longer lists which many people completed in order to arrive at an agreed selection. Marrage was given an arbitrary score of 50 and everyone had to place other events in relation to it. Bereavement was recognized as a source of considerable stress with 'death of a spouse' being ranked as the most stressful life event with a score of 100. 'Death of a close family member' was given a score of 63 and 'death of close friend' scored 37. Respondents were asked to tick off events that had occurred within a specified period, usually one to two years. Originally the score on the scale was simply summed to give a total number of 'life change units', but later attempts were made to weight events. There was an assumption that the events in themselves were not necessarily stressful but that it was the resultant life changes which were challenging. Overall, research findings have revealed only a low correlation between life events and subsequent ill health.

Ogden (1996) highlighted five major flaws in this method of conceptualizing stress:

1 the individual's own rating of the event is important;
2 the problem of retrospective assessment;
3 life experiences may interact with each other;
4 what is the outcome of a series of life experiences?
5 stressors may be short-term or ongoing.

In relation to bereavement, Holmes and Rahe's approach to stress has serious inadequacies. In particular the model does not account for the individual meaning given to the death. There is an assumption that spousal bereavement is worse than the loss of a close friend but this might not be the case. As we argued earlier, bereavement is a single event which is likely to have multiple consequences. For example, the death of a father may be sad for an eldest son but his new role as head of the family may bring power, status and wealth. In a case like this, bereavement has both positive and negative consequences and triggers a series of life experiences requiring adjustment. Some changes following a bereavement are short-term, but others – like status change – may be long-term. In addition, the scale may be rated very differently depending upon the time since the loss.

Stimulus-based models of stress, like response-based models, have their origins in an engineering conceptualization. People are assumed to show the effects of certain levels of strain in the way that mechanical structures, like bridges, do. Is this a reasonable way to understand people? An alternative approach has been developed by Lazarus and Folkman (1984) which takes account of psychological factors in the appraisal and response to stress. It is this approach which underpins the more recent bereavement model proposed by Stroebe and Schut (1996) which is explored in depth in Chapter 5. An important aspect of the Lazarus and Folkman model is the emphasis placed on coping.

The theoretical development of stress and coping can be traced to the earlier work of Lazarus (1996), in which he proposed that stress has three components:

1 primary appraisal – involves determining whether the event represents a threat to that individual;
2 secondary appraisal – involves the process of evaluating the individual coping resources which can be used in response to the threat;
3 coping – involves responding to the threat.

The approach is called a transactional social cognitive model as it encompasses all three elements. Lazarus and Folkman (1984) differentiated between two coping styles: emotion-focused and problem-focused. In emotion-focused coping, the objective is to reduce the feeling of distress or fear associated with the threat. In problem-focused coping, the individual actively seeks ways to mitigate or deal with the threat. It has been proposed that problem-focused coping results in a better outcome as the threat is confronted and dealt with. However, there may be certain situations or types of threat in which emotion-focused coping is the more adaptive response. For example, if the threat engenders very high levels of anxiety, it might be more appropriate for an individual to concentrate on reducing their anxiety level so they can calmly consider their options later, and, of course, some things cannot be changed but people can be comforted. Lazarus and Folkman's model envisages coping responses as being influenced by a number of factors, including usual coping style (e.g. active or passive coping strategies), personality factors (e.g. hardiness, perceived control, self-efficacy), tangible resources (e.g. economic resources), social support, and concurrent life stressors. It appears that problem-focused coping usually predominates when the person believes that action may be helpful, and emotion-focused coping predominates when a person believes that the threat has to be endured.

The transactional model of stress and coping has become very popular but there are a number of criticisms. First, it is very much an individual model which takes little account of social context. People may not have freedom of choice to select from a range of responses, either because they come from cultures which value social cohesiveness over personal autonomy, or because they occupy social roles, such as being a mother, which limit their range of options. Second, the model virtually ignores physiological responses to stress. For example, acutely distressed people may be quite unable to control their emotional responses such as trembling or crying despite cognitively wishing to do so. Finally, there is an emphasis on cognitive processing (appraisal) which takes little account of 'gut-reaction' or habit. The transactional model assumes that people are rational information processors.

Personal characteristics associated with stress

People are very different in how they perceive and experience events, as noted earlier. What makes one person more resilient than another? This section briefly introduces three relatively stable coping styles. There is debate as to the extent to which people are amenable to change following major life events such as loss and bereavement. The theoretical concepts and research largely derive from a western perspective and the values inherent in these societies and therefore they may not be applicable to other cultures.

1 *Perceived control* – Rotter (1966) proposed that individuals vary in how they explain things that happen to them. Some make internal (self) attributions and others external (other people, chance) control attributions. The concept was extended to health care and much research has focused on personal control beliefs. These ideas were further developed by Wallston *et al.* (1978) in the context of attributions made about health and health care services.

2 *Self-efficacy* – is the belief that one can successfully undertake the behaviours which are required for a desired outcome. The concept was originally derived from the work of Bandura (1977) on social learning theory.

3 *Hardiness* – Kobasa (1979) introduced the concept of hardiness which has three components: commitment, control and challenge. A positive belief in one's ability to influence life events, a belief that change is normal and life enhancing, and an active involvement in life are all thought to be protective features.

What are the implications of the stress and coping approach for theories of bereavement?

The stress and coping approach to understanding bereavement has a number of advantages and 'fits' broadly with common-sense ways of understanding bereavement in the western world. We will suggest a number of advantages

---

Advantages of the stress and coping approach

♦ *Accounts for the physical and psychological impact of grief* – this chapter started by describing the physical and psychological consequences of grief. Theoretical models of stress account well for the vast array of problems which can be experienced.

♦ *Integrates psychological and biological factors associated with grief* – a hypothesis which predicts major physiological arousal and the triggering of a 'fight or flight' response following bereavement fits well with the immediate reactions experienced by those people confronted by a sudden unexpected death. Evidence shows that in most people acute reactions diminish over time.

♦ *Increased mortality can be explained to some extent* – there is some evidence that bereaved people have an excess mortality in the first six months following the death. The causes of death may also be associated with stress reactions, if account is taken of the effects on neuroendocrine and immune functioning. Thus existing diseases such as coronary heart disease may be potentiated by biochemical changes such as increased blood viscosity. Likewise immuno-suppression may make people more vulnerable to infections and possibly to cancers.

♦ *Offers an explanation of individual differences* – stress and coping theories, especially the Lazarus and Folkman model, offer an account of why individuals may vary so greatly in their reaction to loss. First, it could be that at the primary appraisal stage, some deaths are not appraised as threatening but merely inevitable, such as those of an elderly relative. Therefore, they do not provoke 'stress' reactions and grieving. Second, even if a death is appraised as threatening, people are predicted to vary in their coping responses by the availability of different coping resources combined with intrinsic (personality) variables. Thus the actual expression of coping is likely to be determined by features of both an individual and their environment.

♦ *Offers suggestions for bereavement support* – the suggestion that individuals may make either emotion-focused or problem-focused coping responses offers first, a conceptual model for categorizing coping endeavours and second, possible interventions. Stroebe (1998) has reported intervention strategies based on these theoretical models which will be presented in the final chapter.

Disadvantages of the stress and coping approach

♦ *Labels responses but does not explain them* – there is a potential danger in labelling responses to grief as stress which then legitimizes no further action being taken. The concept of stress is very confusing and there are few agreed definitions. It is used both as a causal explanation and as an outcome.

♦ *Pathologizes grief* – there may be a tendency to conceive of stress as a 'pathogen' and thus view bereavement as an 'illness' from which people can expect to 'recover'. From this perspective, physiological and psychological reactions are seen as 'symptoms' which should be 'treated'. There is a danger that grief may become medicalized and that people seek pharmacological relief from the suffering which mourning entails. This should not be interpreted to mean that there is never a place for medical care in supporting people by providing information and reassurance and relieving clinical conditions such as anxiety and depression. For example, general practitioners have an important role in recognizing such distress.

♦ *Individualizes grief* – the Lazarus and Folkman model, despite claims to be a social cognitive model, emphasizes individual evaluation of stressful stimuli. This does not adequately account for social influences on mourning and the expression of grief.

♦ *Does not account for cultural constructions* – anthropological evidence demonstrates remarkable variability in human reactions to bereavement. Stress models suggest that there should be more homogeneity of response.

♦ *May be ethnocentric* – the Lazarus and Folkman model could be criticized for being ethnocentric by suggesting that western values of individual autonomy are central to coping. Psychological theories which propose that perceptions of personal control are 'healthy' may not be applicable to cultures in which conformity to social roles and respect for tradition are highly valued.

♦ *Makes an assumption that bereavement is a negative 'threat' rather than a normal process* – a stress and coping perspective on bereavement suggests that it is a 'threat' but other constructions may be possible, for example, that death brings release from suffering. Religions offer alternative constructions of death, for example, notions of transference to 'heaven' within Christianity or to further cycles of rebirth in Buddhism. Such transitions may be welcomed by believers. From these perspectives bereavement is viewed as a normal part of the life cycle not as a stressor.

and disadvantages at this stage but a more thorough evaluation will be offered in the final chapter.

Summary

♦ Grief reactions can encompass physiological, emotional, cognitive, behavioural, sexual and spiritual changes. These reactions vary in disruptiveness and duration.
♦ Bereavement can impact on health. There is evidence of excess mortality and morbidity following bereavement.
♦ Possible physiological and psychological mechanisms which may account for the increased mortality and morbidity have been considered, including the effects of stress on immunity.
♦ Two theoretical models of stress and coping have been presented, the stressful life events approach (Holmes and Rahe 1967) and the transactional model of stress and coping (Lazarus and Folkman 1984).
♦ The advantages and disadvantages of a stress and coping approach to understanding bereavement have been discussed.

Further reading

Bartlett, D. (1998) *Stress*. Buckingham: Open University Press.
Parkes, C.M. (1996) *Bereavement*, 3rd edn. London: Routledge (Chapter 2).
Parkes, C.M., Laungani, P. and Young, B. (eds) (1997) *Death and Bereavement Across Cultures*. London: Routledge (Chapter 4).
Stroebe, M.S. and Stroebe, W. (1987) *Bereavement and Health*. Cambridge: Cambridge University Press (Chapter 2).
Stroebe, M.S., Stroebe, W. and Hansson, R.O. (eds) (1993) *Handbook of Bereavement*. Cambridge: Cambridge University Press (Chapters 2, 10 and 12).

Theoretical perspectives on the family

... society delegates its most crucial functions to the family ...
(Herbert 1988: 16)

In this chapter, literature on the role of the family in shaping responses to loss is be considered. First, the context of family systems research is introduced, then changes and variations in the concept 'family' are highlighted and models of family functioning described, together with a commentary about theoretical and methodological difficulties in the 'systems' approach. We then focus on research studies concerned with families and loss and conclude with an overview of the current status and a look to the future. This is not a comprehensive review of research in family functioning; rather it is an attempt to introduce some of the major issues in this complex area of study.

It is a surprising fact that most models of bereavement, and a substantial portion of writing and research about bereaved people, fail to take the individual's immediate social context – the family – into account. The family is characteristically the primary provider of socialization, social control and support, and as such will have a profound influence on the way its members deal with significant life events. Researchers (for example, Lehman *et al.* 1986) have acknowledged the importance of the type and availability of social support as predictors of outcome after bereavement. Rosenblatt (1993) has also reminded us of the importance of significant other people in the way we define, feel about and come to terms with loss, and Smith (1982) has suggested that we might achieve a better understanding of the meaning of loss if we address the ways in which identity is shaped and maintained by interactions with significant others.

Furthermore, Coyne and DeLongis (1986: 458) point out that 'perceptions of social support do not arise *in vacuo*', and we need also to understand the circumstances in which support comes to be perceived as high or low before we can comprehend how these perceptions impact on stress, coping and adaptation. This plea for the transactional nature of social support to be acknowledged and incorporated into research and theory-building is, of course, highly relevant to studies of family interactions and loss. Such studies as there are, however, have tended to consider one aspect of perceived family functioning, such as family environment or style (e.g. Kissane *et al.* 1998) or boundaries (Boss and Greenberg 1984). This is also true of a number of studies focused on other types of loss such as those associated with acquired disability or chronic or terminal illness: for example, Cormack (1996) on spinal cord injury, Kissane *et al.* (1994) on cancer and Stuifbergen (1990) on chronic illness. These studies tend to show an association between the psychological health of some family members and, for example, self-reported indices of constructs such as family conflict or cohesiveness, but they leave many questions unanswered about the way such constructs develop and about the causal direction of the associations.

Gotay (1996) has commented on the lack of theories or models to guide research on families, and thus the difficulties of choosing appropriate hypotheses to test and measures and analyses to use, and predicting behaviour so that preventive interventions may be designed – and this applies no less to bereavement than to other areas of study. A major barrier to the study of family interaction lies in the difficulty inherent in attempting to identify and account for all the salient variables. A reductionist approach cannot capture the dynamic, multifactorial nature of family life adequately, for all that it may generate testable hypotheses. More holistic qualitative approaches have been slow in coming, and this may in part be related to their costliness in terms of time and resources.

Coyne and DeLongis (1986) argue that existing survey methods need to be supplemented by in-depth interviews and daily diaries. This argument is also advanced by Fisher *et al.* (1990) who consider four problems which have bedevilled family theory and its application to health research:

1 the difficulty in translating family concepts to empirical research;
2 the confusion and uncertainty in measuring 'wholes' and 'parts' of a family;
3 the apparent conflict between circular-causal and linear-causal perspectives in model building;
4 the implicit violation of a family perspective in certain study designs and methods of data analysis.

Fisher *et al.* address the ongoing debate about the relative merits of self-report and observation as methods of data collection, and, like Coyne and DeLongis, argue for the employment of multidimensional assessment strategies:

> the classical dictum of empirical science that reduction and control lead to discovery and understanding . . . is not wholly applicable within family research . . . although scientific rigour needs to be maintained, it is the emergent non-deterministic complexity of the family that needs to be addressed.
>
> (Fisher *et al.* 1990: 188)

Sadly, the use of innovative methods and procedures in the enrichment of family research is still the exception rather than the rule.

Vetere and Gale (1987) and Tutty (1995) have reviewed the theoretical and practical issues in selecting a measure of family functioning. Vetere and Gale argue for a rich and detailed multi-method approach; their naturalistic enquiry used observation and repertory grids, and also films of some family activities and reflective reports by some of the families in an attempt to sample 'family life in the raw, and describe it in its natural vividness' (1987: 11) from both insider and outsider perspectives. Repertory grid constructs were derived from observers' diaries and taped family discussions, and issues of inter-rater reliability and validity were addressed. Few if any researchers have since undertaken studies so ambitious and detailed in their scope. Most have used single methods of enquiry such as questionnaires or repertory grids, or interviews plus standard questionnaires. An exception is the circumplex model presented by Olson *et al.* (1979) of marital and family functioning, which has both observational and self-report components.

Nadeau (1998) used interviews to develop a grounded theory of family meaning-making about death, which will be described in more detail later, and Gale and Barker (1987) used a questionnaire based on constructs derived from the distance regulation theory of Kantor and Lehr (1975) to explore the organization of constructs of self and others in families. This approach enables exploration of perceived similarities and differences between family members and inspection of the construct analyses to investigate why the differences might exist. Thus 'alliances and conflictual groupings can be revealed' (Gale and Barker 1987: 363) as the method allows investigation of the extent to which perceptions are shared by subgroupings within the family, and concepts such as engagement/disengagement and cohesion can be explored. Gale and Barker do not, however, address Coyne and DeLongis' (1986) concerns about the circumstances in which such perceptions arise.

Self-assessment tools are the most commonly used methods of enquiry about family functioning, but concerns about how well such instruments can capture the complexities and dynamic nature of family life remain. Tutty (1995) highlights many such concerns in his detailed review of six of the best-known self-assessment tools: the Family Adaptability and Cohesion Evaluation Scale (FACES-II); the Family Environment Scale (FES); the Family Assessment Device (FAD); the Family Assessment Measure (FAM-III); the Index of Family Relations (IFR) and the Self-report Family Inventory (SRI). Tutty raises concerns about the psychometric properties of most of the scales, and the fact that some (for example the FAD) produce amalgamated scores derived from descriptions of the family by each individual. In those cases, *differences* in how individuals perceive the family, which may be crucial in understanding family functioning, are treated as 'noise' in the analysis, and lost. This is a particular cause for concern in bereavement research, as evidence suggests that family roles and the meanings bound up in those roles (who is being grieved, and by whom) have different kinds of impact for different dyads. A deceased woman may be grieved as a mother, a partner, a sister or a daughter by members of her family, and to blur those differences into one measure of 'family style' as some scales do, is to run the risk of overlooking vital data. Some of the scales, however, do permit examination of particular dyads within the family – for example the FAM-III.

Tutty (1995) also comments on the lack of norms for different genders and different stages of the family life cycle, and the fact that most of the scales preclude children under the age of 12. These three variables, gender, children and family life span, impact on, and are impacted by, bereavement. They have all, separately, been the subject of studies and writings around grief and the family. Gender differences in grieving have been explored by Stroebe (1998). Stroebe discusses the relative vulnerability to health risks of widowed men compared to women, in some cultures, and relates it to gendered differences in expressiveness of emotions. Gelcer (1983) points to the variability in children's expressions of grief, and discusses it in relation to a number of factors including their developmental stage (and thus ability to conceptualize death) and their relationship with the deceased. Normand et al. (1996) also delineated different types of connections children construct to the deceased, and the trajectories of those connections over time. Finally, attributes such as 'cohesion' are not necessarily fixed at one level throughout the family's life cycle; they may be responsive to a range of changes such as the growing independence of young adults who once were children, or to perceptions of external threat if the neighbourhood changes. The adaptive capacity of family attributes cannot be assessed adequately unless measures are taken at more than one point in time.

Hill's (1966) ABCX model of family reactions to stressful life events is unusual in that it attempts to assess adjustment over time; it considers the interaction between stressors and family resources, and includes concurrent and cumulative stressors and their role in long-term adjustment.

Tutty's (1995) review ends with a plea for the development of norms for single-parent and step-families, and families from different ethnic and socioeconomic groups. The lack of norms for groupings other than the traditional western nuclear family highlights one other major difficulty in family research: the concept 'family' does not follow one pattern, nor is it set in stone. Families exist in a variety of forms in different cultures and subcultures, and moreover they change as societies change and new demands and challenges are encountered.

The family: theme and variations

Even today, in societies characterized by rapid change and mobility, the family in one form or another is a significant factor in psychological development and social life. Most people live with or are closely connected to their immediate biological relatives, and many of those who are not will associate closely or cohabit in family-like groups. What then is a family? It is often defined by blood ties and cohabitation, as in: 'the body of persons who live in one house or under one head, including parents, children, etc.' or rather more loosely as 'the unity formed by those who are nearly connected by blood or affinity' (the *Oxford English Dictionary*, second edition, 1989). This looser definition is appropriate in many contemporary western societies, in which the traditional nuclear family of a married couple and their biological children has many variations, and also in the extended families characteristic of many eastern cultures.

Traditionally, in the West, the model of the nuclear family (biological parents and children) or extended nuclear family (parents, children and grandparents) living together is the norm. Herbert (1988: 17) has described 'heightened emotional intimacy and interdependence' as characteristic of these small family groups. However, the concept of the family changes through time in societies undergoing change. The 'typical' western nuclear family who live together until the children are grown has many contemporary variations. High rates of divorce, increasing incidences of lone parenthood, advances in the control of fertility, liberalization of attitudes to homosexual partnerships, all mean that the contemporary nuclear family may be configured in a variety of ways: around step-parents and siblings, single-sex parents (one or two), and with or without formal marriage.

In some cultures, for example, those typically found in some Asian countries, the notion of family may extend to a wide range of those related by blood and marriage ties, and may include 'cousins' who come from the same village or who may claim kinship because of old friendship ties. Segal (1991) has outlined some fundamental characteristics of traditional extended Asian families which are in contrast to those of the typical nuclear families of western Europe. Segal points out the group-focused or allocentric nature of many Asian cultures (in contrast to the individual-focused west). In such cultures, obligation, conformity, obedience and generational interdependence are highly valued, whereas in the West it may be said that individualism, independence and self-sufficiency are goals to be striven for. In other parts of the world, for example among the Maori of New Zealand, yet other patterns of the extended family group exist which have at their core the grandparents-grandchildren relationship.

Chilman *et al.*'s (1988) definition of a family is centred on the importance of *committed relationships* which give the participants *a sense of identity*. It is helpful here as it highlights the essence of the family without prescribing its form.

The family, then, however it may be configured, is the primary means by which the behaviour and experiences of its members are shaped in ways appropriate to societies' needs, particularly but not exclusively when it is involved in the raising of children. A current and widely accepted way of construing the family is as a system. Much of the work on families as systems comes from family therapy, and therefore the dominant models tend to be clinically rather than empirically derived. The following section in which a systems approach is described and explored should be read with the earlier discussion of the methodological limitations of commonly-used scales in mind.

The family: a systems approach

The family is seen as a dynamic institution in which the elements are individual family members. It is the individuals and their interactions which give the family its particular style, but it is more than the sum of its parts; it has a life and life cycle of its own. Through the family's life cycle, its composition changes. Individual roles change, as do relationships. Robinson (1992: 30) described the family as:

> an influencing, organizing and creative agent . . . a living *system* which is distinct from, yet connected to, the life of its individual members . . . every family adopts its own unique way for structuring the roles, relationships and responsibilities that direct their family life. They each have their own system for handling life's differing crises, emotional upheavals, conflicts and demands. Families affirm, protect and define standards of acceptable behaviour, values and beliefs.

There is an increasing body of literature on the family as a system. Systems theory is adapted from the biological sciences, and has the concepts of interrelatedness and organization at its core (Kazak 1989). Thus, among the basic tenets of systems theory are the following maxims:

♦ systems are composed of interrelated parts;
♦ change in one part is associated with change in all the others;
♦ systems maintain a regular state of balance or homeostasis;
♦ systems maintain a balance of periods of change and stability (Hoffman 1981).

Cormack (1996: 5) summarizes the critical aspects of the family as a system rather more fluidly: it has structure (it is a group of individuals), functioning (there is a pattern of relationships among them), boundaries (which define who is inside and who is outside) and roles for its members.

However, Treacher and Carpenter (1984) have argued that the family is properly regarded as a subsystem. They write of the individual as a member of various social systems of which the most important is often, but not always, the family. They also point out that the family should be considered in terms of its interaction with other systems such as the neighbourhood, schools, health and social services, and so on, so there may be various targets for therapeutic intervention. It seems a self-evident truth that families are influenced by their social and cultural contexts (see, for example, Boss and Greenberg 1984), in particular by the resources available to them and the barriers to those resources (such as financial, geographical, racial and social grouping constraints). Smith (1982), for example, describes studies which have demonstrated a positive association between family adjustment (or 'restabilization') after bereavement and the use of external sources of help, from both individuals and agencies.

Research on and clinical interventions with families have tended to use, or at least to pay lip-service to, a systemic approach. Vetere and Gale (1987) have argued that the concepts and terms borrowed from biology and control engineering need clarifying and defining before they are translated for use in family studies, and have described the requirements for a comprehensive theory of family behaviour which is capable of generating testable hypotheses. They also argue that a family theory must be able to describe and explain a number of complex variables – for example, family structure, dynamics, process and change, the transmission of distress on to individuals, the processes of individuation and differentiation of the members. Family theory should also be able to account for how the family mediates between external environmental events and individual development, and how it copes with the seemingly antithetical functions of stability and change, particularly when viewed from within the family's developmental cycle. Vetere and Gale also include the prediction of health and pathology within the family and the prescription of therapeutic strategies for dealing with family dysfunction in their list of requirements for a family theory (1987: 27).

It is clear that many of the models derived from work with families fail to meet the criteria of a comprehensive systems theory. There are many problems in capturing and assessing the complexities and dynamics of family functioning, as has been discussed, but nevertheless several useful constructs have been derived and developed, and studies have produced both descriptive and predictive models of family functioning around dying and bereavement. It is to these that we now turn.

Constructs of family functioning

There is variation in the number and type of constructs used by researchers on families. Among those properties considered by many researchers to be central to descriptions of family functioning are the following:

- *cohesion* – connectedness-separation of family members to and from each other (from enmeshed through connected, separated and disengaged);
- *boundaries* – divide the 'system' from the environment; rules prescribe who is in and how they participate;
- *adaptability* – how the balance between the tendency towards homeostasis and the capacity for change is maintained;
- *homeostasis* – maintenance of a steady state;

♦ *openness* – family members have a high level of exchange with the outside community;
♦ *closedness* – family members have a low level of exchange with the outside community;
♦ *feedback* – the transmission of information about performance so that it can be modified as necessary (Vetere and Gale 1987).

Others have suggested additions to these constructs; for example (Johnson 1988) argues that the following properties are important in adaptive family functioning:

♦ a clear separation of generations;
♦ flexibility in and between roles;
♦ direct and consistent communication;
♦ tolerance of individualism.

Robinson (1992) has also suggested consideration of:

♦ powerlessness;
♦ ambivalence;
♦ interdependence;
♦ uncertainty;
♦ role restructuring;
♦ resiliency;
♦ disturbance of future plans;
♦ alteration of external reference groups.

Robinson's model was developed to consider a family facing cancer, but many of its features are also applicable to bereavement.

Kazak (1989) has also called for consideration of the timeline of adaptive processes: the 'highs and lows' as stressors impinge; how crises are resolved; how the meaning and demands of critical events change with the development of the family as well as the development of the situation or changes in the individual at the core of it. Normand *et al.* (1996), for example, describe different trajectories in children's grief and Eiser (1990) has discussed the roles of stages of cognitive development and experience in shaping children's understanding of death. Worden and Silverman (1996) showed evidence of acute depression-like symptoms in bereaved children soon after the loss, which usually attenuated by the first anniversary and which are regarded as part of a normal reaction, but some children had significant emotional and behavioural problems (social withdrawal, anxiety, social problems) which did not become apparent until two years after the death. Rubin (1984) compared recently-bereaved (3–10 months) and longer-bereaved (2–6 years) mothers who lost babies to Sudden Infant Death Syndrome (SIDS) with non-bereaved controls, and found long-term changes in the meaning and management of the parents' significant relationships after the period of acute grief.

Rubin (1993) also studied parents bereaved of adult children 4 years or 13 years earlier. The children were soldiers killed during war, and, as in the SIDS study, there was a group of non-bereaved controls. Rubin found behavioural, emotional, cognitive and somatic effects persisting over many years in the bereaved groups. In particular, a persistence of high levels of anxiety characterized these groups, leading Rubin to write of 'a permanent shift in the homeostasis of tension regulation post-loss' (Rubin 1993: 296).

Sanders (1989) and Hewson (1997) have also highlighted the importance of considering changes through time in studies of grief. Sanders talks of 'the network of aftershocks' which can disturb the family system in the months and years after a death, and she points out that they are not always understood by survivors to be related to the death. Hewson's episodic stress response model of grief points to the variability of behaviours in response to changing demands and coping capacities over time. The model is based on the stress-appraisal-coping model of Lazarus and Folkman (1984), but Hewson also distinguishes between primary and secondary stress episodes. Primary stress episodes, such as after the death of a family member, arise from the 'extreme emotional and practical demands' made because 'everyday life and expectations for the future are radically changed' (Hewson 1997: 1135). Secondary stress episodes are periods in which the stresses are appraised as not in themselves challenging to everyday life; rather they arise from an accumulation of daily difficulties which undermine the individual's coping resources – lack of sleep, lack of support, and so on. Thus, the stress thresholds are not static; they vary with time and events. They may also vary with gender and/or role (as Rubin 1993 also found). Hewson points to studies which show that, in families dealing with loss in the form of having a disabled child, recurrent stress patterns are more evident in mothers than fathers, for example. Hewson describes her model as descriptive and non-pathological; she points out that recurrent episodes of stress are to be expected in dealing with significant loss. This raises the question of when behaviour in individuals or families should be regarded as pathological. Many of the constructs suggested by family researchers are bipolar, and there is an assumption that the extremes (e.g. enmeshed, distant) are maladaptive.

However, Kazak (1989) has drawn attention to the fact that at times of crisis the family may put its efforts into holding onto a steady state, which may appear as overprotectiveness and enmeshed relationships. These behaviours, which may seem maladaptive from the outside, may function to maintain a protective homeostasis for the family. This effort to maintain homeostasis might also be reflected in other findings. Kissane and Bloch (1984) reviewed the literature on family grief, which is largely based on case reports and observations. Recurring themes in the studies reviewed were inhibition, concealment and lack of communication. It is common to think of these patterns as pathological, as well they might be in some situations, but they may also serve as effective ways of managing family stress. Bonanno *et al.* (1995) have pointed to the possible adaptive value of avoiding unpleasant emotions during grief. Raphael (1984) identified bereaved families typified by resistance to change, low role flexibility and the concealment of distress; and Davies *et al.* (1986) described families as showing 'dysfunctional coping' after losing a child, typified as blocking discussion, suppressing feelings of grief and concentrating on concrete events such as the funeral arrangements. However, it is premature to describe any of these patterns as dysfunctional because they appear extreme during a time of great crisis, as Kazak (1989) has suggested – correct or 'functional' patterns of behaviour cannot be described without relating them to outcome. The following studies on families and grief have attempted to address the connection between family behaviour patterns and outcome in terms of the psychological health of family members.

Family studies and grief

With the difficulties inherent in a systems approach in mind, as we have discussed, the following studies are presented. None has attempted to fulfil the requirements delineated by Vetere and Gale (1987) and Coyne and DeLongis (1986); rather, they have tended to use unidimensional approaches based on self-report by sets of questionnaires or interviews. They cannot therefore be said to have taken a wholly systemic approach, although they may yet have generated some useful data.

Kissane *et al.* (1994) carried out a series of studies on family functioning and grief. They looked at family functioning and psychological morbidity in the families of palliative care patients. They assessed levels of cohesiveness, conflict and expressiveness (FES) and cohesion and adaptability (FACES-III) in attempting to develop a family typology, and used the Beck Depression Inventory (BDI) and Brief Symptoms Inventory (BSI) to measure psychological morbidity. They identified five classes of family style:

1 supportive (high cohesiveness);
2 resolved conflict effectively;
3 hostile (high conflict);
4 sullen (moderate conflict, poor cohesion, limited expressiveness);
5 intermediate levels of cohesion, expressiveness and conflict ('ordinary').

They showed a relationship between family style and the psychological health of family members. Family types 1 and 2 showed low psychological morbidity; 3 and 4 had higher levels of morbidity and poorer social functioning; 5 showed moderate levels of morbidity.

Using a similar method, Kissane *et al.* (1996) studied patterns of family functioning in adult families after the death of a parent, again with the FES and FACES-III, the BDI and BSI, and the BPQ (Bereavement Phenomenology Questionnaire) to assess grief. Families were assessed at six weeks post-bereavement, and followed up at six months and 13 months. Respondents completed the questionnaires independently. The same five types of family as in the previous study were identified at six weeks and six months, and reduced to four types at 13 months when the sullen and intermediate types were indistinguishable. Otherwise, the types were consistent across the three time points. Levels of cohesiveness and conflict made significant contributions to each type, whereas expressiveness was only occasionally relevant and adaptability played no role in discriminating between types.

In the supportive and conflict-resolving families, grief tended to wane over the 13 months and psychosocial outcome was good. In the hostile and sullen families outcome was poor, with sullen families showing high rates of depression and hostile families having 'fractured and chaotic adaptation' (Kissane *et al.* 1998: 15). From these results, Kissane *et al.* (1998) developed a model of family grief therapy, designed to promote healthy family functioning during palliative care and bereavement. They used the Family Relations Index (FRI) derived from the short form of the FES to classify families with a member in palliative care as at high or low risk of poor outcome after bereavement, and piloted a preventive programme with 15 families in the hostile, sullen and intermediate categories. They used focused, time-limited therapy designed to enhance cohesiveness, conflict resolution and the expression of thoughts and feelings, to promote the sharing of grief, and raise awareness of typical patterns of coping with problems or relating to each other. Unfortunately, the attrition rate was high and their results are presented in a very oblique fashion. One is left to draw the conclusion that some families were helped and others were not. The intermediate families, it is suggested, fared better than the hostile ones. Kissane *et al.* (1998) point out that the model is evolving and this was a preliminary study.

Bonanno *et al.* (1995) challenged the notion that emotional avoidance is necessarily maladaptive in their study of mid-life conjugal bereavement. Their study was carried out on the survivor of the married couple and no other family members were sampled, so in that sense this was not a study of family functioning, but the results are interesting here for two reasons: they call into question a widely-held belief, namely that emotional avoidance during bereavement leads to prolonged or delayed symptoms of grief; and they highlight the importance of considering individual differences in behaviour patterns and their relationship to outcome. Individual differences are typically ignored in family studies, or they disappear in among the mean scores, but their contribution to outcome might well be significant.

Ford (1983) wrote of the 'implicit and multidimensional' family rules which provide the connection between family processes and individual behaviour. Book (1996) used a symbolic interactionist approach – an exploration of how the constructions of events used by family members relate to their responses to the events – in her investigation of theories about rules and silences, to explore the impact of family narratives and discussions on the ability of adults to talk about death. She points out that although families often have a rich collection of 'stories' (of family events) to draw on, many adults report that there was little or no discussion about death when they were children. Book interviewed three women, and found that in each case the family had exerted powerful influences on communication about death. Communication took place through silences and impressions as well as talk, and Book stresses the importance of what was *not* said. A small-scale, qualitative study such as Book's is the antithesis of the large-scale surveys characteristic of Kissane *et al.*'s research, yet it provides a number of potentially valuable insights into individual/family interactions, and points to areas for further investigation.

Nadeau (1988) also used a symbolic interactionist approach in her grounded theory analysis of how families make sense of death. She collected her data from interviews (or rather, 'guided conversations') with adult members of bereaved families, in order to explore how people make sense of their world and their experiences and how they learn values and meanings from their interactions with others. Nadeau explored a rich variety of factors in family meaning-making, among them the family members' willingness to talk to each other about the death, those meanings on which two or more members agree, and consensus or complete agreement about a meaning attached to the death. She found that families most willing to talk to each other about the death tended to have attributes such as tolerance of each others' point of view, frequent interactions and many family and funeral rituals. Those who were least willing to talk tended to have fragile family ties, previous conflicts and divergent beliefs.

Lantz and Ahern (1998) describe 're-collection' in psychotherapy with families dealing with death, in which the client family is helped to remember and honour past events which have special meaning. They talk of this process as helping to 'shrink the family meaning vacuum and those symptoms and problems that grow and flourish' (p. 4) within such a vacuum. A meaning vacuum occurs when family members are not able to discover and experience a sense of meaning and purpose in life (because of facing the death of one of their number). The therapy aims to help people notice meaning potentials and opportunities for the future, to discover actualizing opportunities in the present, and 're-collect' and honour events from the past by means such as recounting stories, using art, poetry or photographs in order to show pride in the life and achievements of their loved one. This was essentially a clinical study, and unfortunately lacked formal baseline or outcome measures, but improvement was reported; participants 'felt good' after the intervention.

Through all these studies with their diverse methodologies and approaches runs the common thread of the importance of facilitating communication about the deceased member and about feelings. All the families described as dysfunctional seem to share inhibited or avoidant expression of their thoughts and feelings, although as we have seen, the time post-loss at which the families were sampled, and the persistence of the behaviours, may be salient in determining whether those patterns are pathological or protective. Interventions aimed at facilitating communication seem to have mixed and not very impressive results. This may suggest that where such a family style is entrenched, it is serving a purpose for the group or for one or more of its members which may not be obvious to an outsider, and in which the others are colluding. Such families may have members with poor psychological health – perhaps the needs of the family do indeed override those of the individuals, especially at times of crisis.

Another characteristic of family studies, as indicated by Tutty (1995) is their relative neglect of children. Nadeau's (1997) in-depth exploration of family meanings is a fascinating document, but she chose to exclude children under 18. She reports that two children insisted on being interviewed, but that their contributions were not included in the analysis. Indeed, studies on the impact of family bereavement on children are few, and results from the small number of studies on interventions are inconclusive (see Stokes *et al.* 1997). The impact of children's presence, needs and grief on other family members during bereavement is not known. It may be that obtaining reliable accounts of feelings and events from children is considered to be problematic, and Stokes *et al.* (1997) have drawn attention to the methodological and ethical difficulties in evaluating interventions, but these issues should be regarded as challenges to investigators, not insurmountable barriers. The fact that children do not behave like adults when they grieve has led to the old lay belief that they do not feel loss so deeply or for so long, and that they are therefore unlikely to be adversely affected in the long term, but it has long been known that these beliefs are erroneous, as the studies cited here show. Further, there is a well-established link between adult depression and childhood bereavement (see, for example, Raphael 1984). The challenges to researchers posed by children's grief and those posed by family functioning are essentially the same. There is a need to establish models of the processes involved which are sensitive, dynamic and predictive.

Summary

♦ Families are variously configured but share the common characteristics of committed relationships which give participants a sense of identity (Chilman *et al.* 1988); they are thus the primary means of social support and socially shaped behaviour in societies.

♦ It has become common to talk of family 'systems', although to date models of family functioning cannot be said to encompass a wholly systemic approach.

♦ Assessment of family style or environment by self-report is the means by which most studies have approached description and prediction of family functioning.

◆ Variables such as gender, life-span stage, family composition and changes through time need to be incorporated into family studies in order to improve their precision and thus their usefulness.

Further reading

Nadeau, J.W. (1997) *Families Making Sense of Death Dysfunction*. Thousand Oaks, CA: Sage. A grounded theory analysis of family meaning-making in bereaved families with adult children, which contains a brief selective review of other important and contemporary work in the field.

CHAPTER
4

Theoretical perspectives: life span development

This chapter aims to introduce a different perspective on loss and bereavement from the previous chapters. We will be considering theories which are variously classified as coming from life span, developmental or psychosocial transitions perspectives. These are based on an assumption that there are normal patterns in human life cycles in which there is, as the Bible says, 'a time to be born and a time to die'. Therefore, change or transitions are regarded as a normal part of human experience; unless we die very young, we can all expect to encounter loss and bereavement. These experiences may lead to psychosocial development and growth as people adjust to new circumstances and learn how to cope with loss, change and grief. This approach to understanding loss also touches on major theoretical debates within psychology including the extent to which there is continuity or discontinuity within development, and the nature-nurture debate. We consider the impact of deaths that occur at different periods of the life cycle, from deaths at the beginning of life such as miscarriage, stillbirth and neonatal death to those occurring in old age.

Arguably, the theories of three major contributors – Sigmund Freud, John Bowlby and Colin Murray Parkes – have been most influential in determining how bereavement and grief are currently conceptualized. In this chapter, we briefly describe the relevant aspects of Freud's work related to understandings of loss. The majority of the chapter, however, concentrates on examining Bowlby's theory of 'attachment and loss' and Parkes' conceptually-related research and theory of psychosocial transitions. Bowlbys' and Parkes' ideas have informed notions of 'normal' and 'pathological' grief, and their theories are widely used by those who seek to help and support the bereaved. It is only relatively recently that some of the basic assumptions underlying these theories have been challenged and new directions identified.

The chapter ends with a review of the evidence in support of a life span perspective. Mention is also made of other contributors to this field including the work of Peter Marris. Chapter 5 will deal in more depth with theories and therapeutic methods with have developed over the last 30 years. This leads on to a critical analysis of the basic postulates of these models which are also discussed in Chapter 5.

Life span perspectives

Before considering the main theories in detail, it may be helpful to consider the key aspects which are emphasized in this approach to understanding loss.

Social relationships

A most basic observation is that human beings are essentially social animals. We live in social groups: families, communities, villages, towns and cities (as discussed in Chapter 3 on family issues in bereavement). In fact, living an isolated existence is normally considered to be rather 'odd' and solitary confinement is used as a punishment. How and why do people form relationships with each other? What happens when relationships end? We noted in the last two chapters that social relationships, in the form of social support, may enhance health.

Change is normal

A common assumption is that change is a basic aspect of life. Physiologically and psychologically people are not static but in a constant state of flux. Parkes (1971, 1993b) suggests that a major determinant of mental health is how people construe change. If changes are seen as purely negative events, rather than as positive or a combination of both aspects, they present a greater challenge to the adaptive capacity of an individual.

Emphasis on early experience

As we will discuss later, it is a widely held belief that early childhood experiences influence adult life. It is suggested that early childhood experiences, especially relating to the formation of social relationships, provide patterns or templates for subsequent relationships and influence the development of personality. Thus unsatisfactory or damaging experiences in early childhood are likely to have long-term consequences. Animal research provides some support for this argument in other species (e.g. Hofer 1996). This may lead to the unfortunate conclusion that all development stops after childhood and the prospect for adults, especially older adults, is a series of decrements in ability and capacity. A dismal picture is unlikely to be the case, and theories such as Erikson's (1963) psychosocial stages propose a life span approach. Erikson developed an eight-stage model of psychosocial development which he derived from psychoanalytic theory. He emphasized that at each stage of development there are special issues that must be confronted (called crises) before development can proceed successfully.

Continuity-discontinuity

There is also a long-standing debate within developmental psychology about the extent to which development proceeds as a continuous process versus the view that development is best characterized as a series of sequential but qualitatively different stages.

Nature-nurture

Another long-standing debate, which it is appropriate to mention briefly, concerns the extent to which human behaviour is genetically determined (nature) versus patterned by environmental stimuli (nurture) such as education and social circumstances. Neither extreme is likely to be correct, and perhaps it is most helpful to envisage nature and nurture as a continuum along which genetic endowment sets the limits in which environmental factors act.

The timeliness of death

There are common-sense notions in most societies about when it is appropriate in the life cycle to die. Some deaths violate those assumptions and have been found to be particularly problematic, such as the deaths of young adults. In contrast, there is an expectation that older people, especially the very old, will die soon. There are assumptions that death will occur in the older, rather than the younger generations of a family, so it may be particularly sad for grandparents and parents to lose a child (Riches and Dawson 1997). Untimely deaths have been acknowledged as a potential risk factor in poor bereavement outcome (Sanders 1993).

Miscarriage, stillbirth and neonatal deaths represent types of death that have not always been acknowledged by society (Lovell 1997). While they may be keenly felt by the parents, they are rarely accorded the full ritual of an adult death. In fact, miscarriage in early pregnancy is relatively common. In previous centuries, with high rates of stillbirth and neonatal death, it might have been an adaptive mechanism of society not to fully acknowledge the status of its youngest members. This has been used to account for the absent or reduced mourning rituals associated with such losses, for example, by the Jewish faith (Levine 1997). More recently, there has been a change in the way late miscarriage and stillbirth have been handled by the medical and midwifery professions. Parents are now offered the option of seeing and holding their dead baby and there is a growing awareness that mementoes such as photographs, hand prints and clothing may be treasured by parents as reminders of their child that did not survive but is still part of their family. Some hospitals offer regular memorial services that acknowledge parents' grief. It may be difficult for other family members and friends to share the loss and grief as they never knew the baby as a person, however they may be able to understand the meaning of the loss, particularly if there has been a history of prior miscarriages. Susan Hill (1989) provides a moving, personal account of the loss of her daughter, Imogen, shortly after birth.

In late twentieth-century Britain and the USA, the death of a child is a relatively unusual event but widely regarded as deeply tragic (Klass 1996). However, it is a much more common experience for parents in other parts of the world and it should not be assumed that they are any less affected by grief because of its frequency.

Childhood death challenges assumptions about continuity of generations and robs parents of plans for the future. There is some evidence that mothers and fathers grieve in different ways which may give rise to marital difficulties (Schwab 1992). Klass (1996) has described how some parents adapt to the loss of children with the assistance of a worldwide self-help group, The Compassionate Friends. These parents derive support from each other in their shared experience of loss.

Many children experience the death of a parent during childhood. There is considerable controversy concerning the impact of death on children (Harrington and Harrison, 1999). Many theoretical models of psychopathology and grief are based on assumptions that childhood bereavement will cause lasting impact on psychological development (these models will be presented later in this chapter and in the following chapters). Of course, the actual impact of bereavement may relate to the circumstances of the loss (sudden versus expected), the developmental age of the child, the resources of the remaining parent in supporting the child and managing their own grief, and other important factors. Christ (1998) followed up 92 families with children ranging in age from 6–17 years who were participating in a parent guidance intervention both before and after the death. At 14 months after bereavement, 120 out of 142 children were categorized as having a favourable outcome, including doing well in school and out of school activities. Only 17 children were having severe problems and these were associated with poor parenting skills, secondary stressors, bereavement suppression and unresolved family conflict.

It may be that the negative impact of bereavement in childhood is more closely associated with the disruptive events that are likely to co-occur. Some children face the impact of deaths resulting from war situations.

Goldstein *et al.* (1997) documented the impact of war on Bosnian children. They assessed 364 children aged 6–12 years who were internally displaced by the war. Virtually all of the children had traumatic war-related experiences including separation from their family, close contact with fighting and multiple losses through bereavement. Approximately 94 per cent of the children met criteria for a diagnosis of PTSD.

The majority of bereavement research has concentrated on adults, especially those who lose a spouse. There is less evidence about how older people grieve the loss of grandchildren and friends. Assumptions are made that death in old age is timely and to be expected but this may not be how it is experienced by older adults or those close to them. Foster (1998), for example, provides a personal account contrasting the untimely death of her sister-in-law and the death of her father, aged 96 years. The last two years of her father's life in which he was slowly dying were distressing for him and the family and his death was 'shocking' as it seemed he would continue to live for ever. Timeliness may be too unwieldly a concept; what the death means to the individual may be of greater importance.

The contribution of Freud to theories of loss and bereavement

The most influential and earliest theories of bereavement emerged from the psychoanalytic tradition, perhaps the most important being those of Freud (1917), Lindemann (1944), Fenichel (1945) and Sullivan (1956). Freud contributed much to twentieth-century thought, but in this section we will merely summarize his ideas which relate specifically to grief and loss.

In 1917, Freud first pointed out the similarities and differences between grief and depression in his classic text *Mourning and Melancholia*. His paper offered one of the first descriptions of normal and pathological grief. The thoughts discussed in it underpin psychoanalytic theory of depression and provide the base for many current theories of grief and its resolution. In the light of the impact of Freud's theory of grief on subsequent theoretical developments, it is surprising to acknowledge that grief as a psychological process was never Freud's main focus of interest. In *Mourning and Melancholia* he argued that people became attached to others (people or objects) who are important for the satisfaction of their needs and to whom emotional expression is directed. Love is conceptualized as the attachment or cathexis of libidinal energy to the psychological representation of the loved person (sometimes called the love object). It is assumed that the more important the relationship, the greater the degree of cathexis. If the person or object is lost through death, the bereaved person's libidinal energy remains attached to thoughts and memories of the deceased. According to Freudian theory, grieving represents a dilemma because there is a simultaneous need to relinquish the relationship so that the person may regain the energy invested and a wish to maintain the bond with the love object. The individual needs to accept the reality of the loss so that the emotional energy can be released and redirected. The process of withdrawing energy from the lost object is called decathexis or 'grief work'.

From a Freudian perspective four charactistics of 'normal' mourning have been identified:

1 a profoundly painful dejection;
2 a loss of capacity to adopt new love objects;
3 a reduction in activity or a withdrawal of activity not connected with thoughts of the loved person;
4 a loss of interest in the outside world because it does not involve the dead person.

Freud postulated that bereaved people need to engage in repeated reality testing in order to accept that the loss is permanent. He conceptualized that the function of grief was to enable the bereaved person to sever ties with the deceased, which was achieved through gradual detachment involving reviewing the past and ruminating on the lost relationship. He regarded this intra-psychic processing as essential to the breaking of relationship bonds with the deceased, to allow the reinvestment of emotional energy and the formation of new relationships with others. He argued that the task of grief work could not be circumvented if the bereaved person was to avoid the development of pathological grief. Freud believed that grief work was mainly concerned with the removal of the libido from the lost object, and its attachment to a new object. He proposed three elements:

1 freeing the bereaved from bondage to the deceased;
2 readjustment to new life circumstances without the lost person;
3 building new relationships.

Freud saw grief as an emotional and solitary process in which mourners had to withdraw from the world in order to detach. He ignored interpersonal aspects such as the urge to talk to others and the value of doing so. This concentration on relinquishing ties to the deceased in order to facilitate grief and the process of detachment is currently a source of debate among theorists. Klass *et al.* (1996) argue that there are numerous studies which challenge the assumption that the purpose of grief is to sever bonds with the deceased in order to form new relationships. They suggest that the purpose of grief is to maintain a continuing bond with the deceased in such a way as to be compatible with other new and continuing relationships. In an American study of widows, Conant (1996) showed that 'coping well' was attributed to the ability to incorporate the past spousal relationship into their current personalities and maintain a bond.

Early irrevocable loss, such as loss of a parent, is particularly damaging as the young child may have a limited understanding of loss. This may cause self-blame and may be associated with feelings of guilt and self-hatred. This may cause increased vulnerability to depression in adult life as noted by some studies (Brown and Harris 1978).

Freud's work was also influential in defining pathological grief. He proposed three criteria:

1 the presence of hatred for the lost object which is expressed through self-reproach;
2 identification with the lost object through internalization;
3 the disposition of the libido in melancholia to withdraw into the ego, instead of being transferred to a new love object as happens in 'normal' mourning.

A central feature of Freud's theory of pathological mourning is the notion of identification. He originally believed that identification only occurred in pathological grief, but by 1923, he proposed that it was an important aspect of all mourning. In pathological grief, he suggested that the aggressive component of the ambivalent state turns inward and causes depression. However, the repression of aggressive thoughts causes some aspects of grief work to be carried on in the unconscious rather than the conscious. It is proposed that after the lost object is incorporated into the ego by the process of identification, the hostile and aggressive part of the ambivalence which is felt towards the deceased manifests itself in the hatred which is discharged towards the ego in feelings of guilt, self-reproach and self-accusation (Mendelson 1982). This results in depression which results from ambivalence in the relationship with the deceased.

To summarize, Freud emphasized:

◆ the importance of early childhood experiences, believing that the first five years of life was the most important period for the development of the personality;
◆ the differentiation of depression and grief;
◆ the 'grief work' hypothesis, with an emphasis on intra-psychic processes.

Freud's understanding of loss and grief may be challenged because he worked from a psychiatric perspective and most of his theories are based on clinical experiences with depressed people and not on data from normal populations. However, Freud's concept of grief work and the need to confront grief in order to gain detachment has had a powerful and lasting impact on both subsequent theory and clinical practice.

An influential paper was written by Lindemann (1944) based on between eight to ten psychiatric interviews conducted with bereaved relatives of those killed in the Boston Coconut Grove fire (n=13) or in the Second World War (n=88). Based on his clinical experience, he developed a theory in which grief was considered to be a syndrome comprising five elements:

1 somatic disturbance;
2 preoccupation with the image of the deceased;
3 guilt;
4 hostility;
5 disorganized behaviour.

He also identified two patterns of 'abnormal' grief:

1 delay in grief reaction which may last for many years;
2 distorted grief reaction – e.g. isolation, hypochondriacal development of the dead person's symptoms, psychosomatic illness and manic
over-activity.

Lindemann made an important contribution to understandings of
bereavement because he was the first person to describe parameters for
normal and pathological grief such as duration and intensity and the first to
acknowledge changes in social functioning. However, many of the factors
he identified as pathological are now known to be relatively common and
normal experiences during grief.

The contribution of John Bowlby: a theory of attachment, separation and loss

Attachment theory provides an explanation for the common human tendency
to develop strong affectional bonds and a way of understanding the emotional response to the severing of the bonds. Bowlby (1969, 1973, 1980)
believed grief is an instinctive, universal response to separation with the
function of promoting union. He relied on childhood experiences to explain
bereavement reactions in adulthood. His attachment theory emphasizes the
biological, rather than the psychological, function of grief. He argues that
the biological function of grief is to trigger behaviours that are likely to
promote proximity to attachment figures, and that separation from attachment figures is anxiety provoking. This psychological response to loss
was conceptualized as dependent on the nature of the original relationship
between the bereaved and the deceased. Following death this is not possible
and, therefore, the biological response is dysfunctional.

Attachment

There have been a number of different theories about how and why the first
relationship between mother and baby is formed, including behavioural
theories based on a drive-reduction hypothesis or operant conditioning.
However, the most widely accepted theory of early relationships was

proposed by Bowlby (1969). A number of important factors influenced Bowlby's thinking including: psychoanalytic theory, research findings from ethology, his clinical experience working as a psychiatrist and his knowledge of the impact of the Second World War on displaced and orphaned children. From psychoanalytic theory, he adopted ideas about predetermined biological patterns of instinctive behaviour in the newborn infant, such as crying and sucking, and the importance of early childhood development. From ethological research, he was influenced by the concept of imprinting described by Konrad Lorenz (1966), in which greylag geese chicks were observed to form strong attachments to animate objects (usually the mother goose) in the first 24 hours after hatching. This imprinting occurs during a limited period and having occurred, is resistant to change. As this behaviour occurs in other animals, the concept was generalized to human beings and described as 'bonding'. From his clinical work, Bowlby noted that young people who displayed behavioural problems often had a history of disruptive family relationships. His ideas about separation and loss were particularly influenced by accounts of the distress shown by infants and toddlers when separated from their mothers.

According to Bowlby (1969), both infants and mothers have evolved a biological need to stay in constant contact with each other. This ensures survival as human infants are helpless and vulnerable for a relatively long period after birth and need the protection, warmth, food and love provided by a mother (or mother substitute). Bowlby's theory had the following main hypotheses:

♦ there is a sensitive period between birth and 5 years of age which is the optimal time for bonding;
♦ early attachment behaviours such as crying and smiling bring the mother to the infant and later attachment behaviours such as clinging and calling ensure the infant follows or stays in contact with the mother;
♦ the mother or other main caregiver is the primary attachment figure;
♦ infants establish an attachment with one main person;
♦ once the attachment has been formed, the infant will remain attached to that individual.

Attachment is an interactional process based on a social model in which both participants influence the development of the bond. According to Berk (1991) the process of attachment occurs over the first two years of life. The nature of attachment has been the focus of considerable research over the last 20 years. Many of Bowlby's original proposals have been modified – for example, it has been found that children may form a number of other important attachments with their fathers, grandparents and siblings. There is also evidence that not all children form secure attachments and that insecure attachment may be associated with problem behaviours.

Separation

Bowlby (1969) noted that the responses of grieving adults were similar to those of young children following the loss of their mothers. His ideas were much influenced by the work of Robertson (1953) who made a series of harrowing films which revealed the extent and characteristics of distress shown by separated young children. The phases of distress were:

◆ *protest* – marked by anger and loud crying, with constant searching for the lost mother and a hypervigiliance anticipating her return;
◆ *despair* – marked by withdrawal and less vigorous crying;
◆ *detachment* – marked by an outward display of cheerful behaviour while the child remains emotionally distant.

Evidence for these phases was provided by observations of hospitalized children and those in institutional care. At that time hospitals restricted visiting, particularly on children's wards because seeing parents appeared to cause children to become distressed. Even when these children were reunited with their parents, they displayed ambivalent and disturbed behaviours like pushing their mother away, refusing to be held or cuddled, or inappropriate clinging. Moreover, children who had been reared in long-term institutional care or had been subjected to long periods of hospitalization, especially where there had been frequent changes of staff, showed inappropriate social behaviour by approaching strange adults in a superficially friendly manner but not establishing emotional contact with them.

Bowlby (1980) hypothesized that following separation, attachment behaviours have a biological function in ensuring that infants and mothers remain together, and if separated they rapidly seek to be reunited. He suggested that these behaviours had evolved to ensure the survival of children by keeping them in touch with their caregivers. The theory is not restricted to humans, but is a pattern of behaviour which can be seen in many other species, where parental care is necessary for rearing offspring. Bowlby argued that attachment bonds were marked by intense emotional involvement in their formation, maintenance, disruption and renewal following separation: 'The unchallenged maintenance of a bond is experienced as a source of security and the renewal of a bond as a source of joy' (Bowlby 1980: 40). The mere threat of loss of an attachment figure gives rise to anxiety while the actual loss is experienced as sorrow. Bowlby also suggests that anger may be present in these situations.

There has been a considerable body of research which has examined the nature of attachment and investigated 'separation anxiety' using the experimental 'strange situation' (Ainsworth *et al.* 1978). This involves a standardized procedure of time limited separations of the child and mother and the introduction of a new person to the child (for a full description of the procedures see textbooks on developmental psychology, e.g. Berk 1991). Bowlby has argued that children who either fail to form satisfactory attachments or form atypical, unstable attachments, perhaps because of repeated separations in childhood, are more vulnerable to psychopathology in later life.

Irrevocable loss

On the basis of attachment theory, Bowlby conceived of grief and mourning following bereavement as a form of separation anxiety. This was originally proposed as a three phase model, and later developed as a four phase model (further details will be provided in subsequent chapters). Bowlby was careful to emphasize that the phases were not discrete entities and that people may oscillate between phases, although over the course of time it was anticipated that people would move through the phases. Bowlby and Parkes collaborated, influencing the development of each others' ideas and developed a phase model of grief (Bowlby and Parkes 1970). That they were influenced by each others' work is made clear by Parkes (1996: 30), so it is not surprising that there are similarities in their theoretical contributions to understanding grief. Likewise, Bowlby drew heavily on Parkes' empirical studies of widows in developing his ideas about phases of bereavement. The phase model of grief is described in Chapter 5.

Bowlby's theory (1980) made a number of important predictions, the first being that grief responses are triggered by the loss of an attachment figure. The closer and stronger the attachment, the more intense and enduring the distress of grief. He suggests that individuals who lose a spouse, child or close family member will be more likely to display intense grieving responses than those who have lost a distant relative or friend. You may like to reflect on your own experience to test this prediction. However, it may also be worth recalling the responses to the death of Diana, Princess of Wales in 1997. How would you account for these?

Bowlby emphasized the concept of grief work to explain how people resolve loss. He proposed that people cognitively redefined themselves and their situation, and that this was a necessary process of realizing and reshaping internal representations to align them with changes that have occurred. He predicted that grief work was a gradual process.

Attachment theory also makes predictions about the nature of grief responses based on the type of attachments. Those with insecure attachments, such as disorganized, ambivalent or dependent relationships, are predicted to be more vulnerable to complicated or pathological grief. Therefore pathological grief is assumed to result from childhood experiences. Bowlby (1980) hypothesized that there were three disordered forms of attachment in childhood that could increase vulnerability following bereavement:

1 anxious attachment;
2 compulsive self-reliance;
3 compulsive caregiving.

He also described two types of pathological grief: chronic mourning that involved depression alternating with anxiety, and absent grief where prolonged lack of conscious grieving and little evidence of disorganization leaves the person prone to sudden acute depression at a later date. A fuller discussion of pathological grief is provided in the next chapter.

There is some evidence in support of Bowlby's claims from observational studies of children, particularly in support of the hypothesis that individuals become anxious and insecure if their childhoods have been characterized by parental rejection. Typically, children with these histories show frequent and urgent attachment behaviours such as clinging, even when the situation does not appear to warrant them. Bowlby (1980) argued that these children had lost confidence that their attachment figure would be available when needed and that their behaviours can be explained as a strategy for maintaining close proximity. He also assumed that individuals who had experienced anxious attachment in childhood maintained this form of attachment in their spousal relationship. He considered that such people were most likely to present symptoms of chronic grief after a major bereavement. Parkes (1995) provides some evidence in support of these claims that childhood patterns of attachment influence adult grief.

There is less evidence to support Bowlby's ideas about people who have compulsive self-reliant attachments. However, he argued that they may have difficulties in accepting love and care from others and wished to be totally independent (Bowlby 1980). Bowlby argued that this attachment style also resulted from ambivalent parenting with children reacting by inhibiting attachment feelings and behaviours, and disclaiming any desire for close relationships. Bowlby thought that following bereavement, self-reliant people were likely to deny the loss and delay grief work, resulting in strain, irritability and depression.

In his third group, compulsive care-giving, there is no empirical evidence to support Bowlby's ideas. He proposed that people in this group can engage in relationships but only as a giver and not as a receiver of care. The antecedents of this attachment style are thought to arise from the childhood experience of an ill, unavailable or disabled mother with the child required to take on the caregiving role to either the mother or other members of the family such as siblings. People in this group are thought to be prone to chronic grief.

It would seem that attachment theory predicts that those who have experienced a happy and fulfilling marriage may find it easier to adjust to widowhood than those who have had an unhappy, or unfulfilled, relationship. It also explains why some people may be affected by the loss of family members with whom they are no longer close. For example, following a difficult divorce or marital separation, children may lose touch with one parent. However, when that parent dies, perhaps many years later, they may experience feelings of guilt, anger and conflict and be uncertain about how to mourn the loss.

Focus on research

The role of loneliness and social support in adjustment to loss – a test of attachment theory versus stress theory (Stroebe *et al.* 1996)

Here we consider one study which sought to test predictions derived from stress theory (which was introduced in Chapter 2) and attachment theory, introduced in this chapter. Stroebe *et al.* (1996) used data from a longitudinal study of widowhood to test two predictions. The first was derived from stress theory and the role of social support in 'buffering' the impact of loss. They developed a deficit model of partner loss which suggested that loss of a partner would lead to deficits in instrumental support, validational support, emotional support and support from social contacts. They predicted that the presence of social support would alleviate the stress of bereavement, but only by the extent to which it replaced the deficits formerly supplied by the spouse. In contrast, attachment theory predicts that attachment figures have a unique status in that they can foster feelings of well-being and security which cannot be substituted by other people in the form of social support. Weiss (1975) discriminated between two forms of loneliness: emotional isolation, which results from the absence of close emotional attachment figures, and social isolation which results from the lack of a social network. He predicted that friends and others could help to alleviate social isolation but not emotional isolation.

The study sampled 60 widowed people (30 men and 30 women) who were matched with 60 married people living in southern Germany. Participants were interviewed three times following bereavement and assessed on self-report measures of perceived social support, loneliness and psychological symptoms. The results demonstrated that people who perceived that they had higher levels of social support reported less depression and fewer physical symptoms than those who perceived the availability of social support to be low. This lends support to attachment theory rather than stress theory. The authors conclude that it suggests that the loss of a partner means losing a major attachment figure, which the social support of family and friends cannot compensate for. This fits well with accounts of bereaved people who say that however well-meaning and kind their families and friends are they cannot, and do not, replace the deceased partner (Young and Cullen 1996). However the type of support may be crucial because support provided by family and friends may vary and much evidence suggests that bereavement can deskill people so that they feel they do not know how to respond. It suggests that emotional loneliness may remain, even when bereaved people appear to be surrounded by others, which has implications for professionals trying to help the bereaved. This must be borne in mind when assessing the need for bereavement care.

Questions remain about how far it is appropriate to infer that attachment behaviours displayed in children are similar to adult mourning behaviours. In evaluating attachment theory, it is clear that it attempts to fill some of the gaps in psychoanalytic theory. According to Bowbly (1980), Freud's (1917) theory failed to account for the nature of the psychological processes in 'normal' mourning, identification with the deceased and the importance of anger. However, in our view, neither Frued's nor Bowlby's theories adequately define the difference between grief work and rumination. This is an important issue as there is evidence that merely ruminating about a death does not promote coping with the loss by the bereaved (Stroebe 1992/3).

Psychosocial transitions: the contribution of Colin Murray Parkes

As well as contributing to the development of attachment theory, Colin Murray Parkes, through his collaboration with Bowlby also proposed that bereavement is a psychosocial transition (Parkes 1971). He suggested that loss threatens inner assumptions about the world and it is this challenge which creates the emotional impact. It is the pain of change and the challenge of readjusting one's taken-for-granted ways of living which lie at the heart of the disruption and distress caused by bereavement.

A central tenet of Parkes' theory is the notion that loss and bereavement challenge the assumptive world. Consequently one of the most important tasks facing bereaved people is to integrate the changes created by the loss into a new or adapted assumptive world. Parkes assumes that individuals have relatively stable, taken-for-granted ways of understanding their world. This allows them to function in relation to others with the minimum of explanation or disruption. It creates a sense of security, stability and continuity. The routine patterns of social interaction are comforting for most people. The more enmeshed the person was with the deceased, the greater the predicted sense of loss. This may account for the acute distress associated with spousal loss. Thus there are likely to be many more changes to a person's everyday life when a partner dies than when a distant relative dies. There are two other predictions which can be made from this theory: first that sudden, unexpected loss is more traumatic than anticipated loss, and second, that untimely loss (those occurring for example in middle life compared to old age) is more upsetting than timely loss.

Parkes suggests that psychosocial transition, that 'inevitably takes time and effort' (1971: 90) follows bereavement and other major life events. At this time individuals are required to modify or change ways of being in the world that were functional before the loss but are now meaningless or redundant without the deceased. For example, formerly shared habits and activities need to be relearned as a single person. Parkes suggests that people need to develop a new identity appropriate to new circumstances. For example, a self-concept which is based on the role of being a wife becomes redundant in widowhood. Important others are needed to play reciprocal roles and their absence means that it is impossible for individuals to have that identity or to play those roles. Readers can imagine what this may mean to a mother whose only child dies. Parkes proposes that there is a period of disorganization where people discover the inadequacy of their previous ways of functioning and this may contribute to the distress and disruption of the early period of bereavement. He regards the process of reorganization as effortful and demanding. He also suggests that people are inherently resistant to change. Moreover, they have to acknowledge the loss and the necessity for change before this can start to occur. So grieving is a time of identity transition. In the creation of a new identity, for example from husband to widower, roles, relationships and cognitive schemata are renegotiated. The bereaved person may also recreate an identity for the deceased. This proposal is more fully developed by Walter (1996) and is discussed in Chapter 5. Parkes provides examples of identification with the deceased, perhaps by becoming more like them in personality or leisure pursuits, or even developing similar symptoms. The outcome of successful grieving is a new identity which integrates the deceased into the life story of the survivor.

Loss and change: the contribution of Peter Marris

There have been other writers who have contributed to the development of theoretical ideas within the overall framework of understanding loss as a psychosocial transition. Some of these developments will be discussed in Chapter 5 and in this section we briefly mention the contribution of Peter Marris. Marris (1992, 1986) saw grief as a process of psychological reintegration impelled by the contradictory desires to recover what has been lost and to escape from painful reminders. He believed that there are two important innate dispositions: the need for attachment and the need to conceptualize. These combine to form habits of feeling, behaviours and perceptions which create structures of meaning enabling adults to predict, interpret and assimilate their environment. Particular relationships, such as partner or parent, become crucial to the formation of meaning in our lives and if such a relationship is lost the whole structure of meaning (or constructs) that centred upon it disintegrates. Grief is the expression of the intense anxiety and despair that this collapse provokes.

Bereaved people adapt by assimilating reality into existing structures of meaning and try to avoid what cannot be assimilated. Grief is also, therefore, the expression of the conflict between the contradictory impulses to preserve all that is valuable, while reestablishing a meaningful pattern of life. Each impulse checks the other and, if aborted or too unchecked, the bereaved person may never 'recover'. Thus grief is mastered not by ceasing to care for the deceased but by abstracting what was fundamentally important in the relationship and rehabilitating it by extricating the essential meaning of the relationship. This contrasts with psychoanalytic and attachment theories, and phase models of grief, all of which emphasize the need to sever emotional ties with the deceased. Marris' observations about the continuing importance of the meaning of the relationship with the deceased have been confirmed by empirical studies of adults (Silverman 1986; Shuchter and Zisook 1993; Marwit and Klass 1995) and bereaved children (Silverman *et al.* 1992).

Summary

♦ Freud differentiated between grief and depression. He introduced the concept of 'grief work' describing the cognitive-emotional processing of information about the loss. He argued that this was necessary before the bereaved person could reinvest emotional energy in others.
♦ Bowlby proposed a theory of attachment and loss. Attachments have evolved to ensure the survival of the young. Attachment relationships are essential for adequate emotional, social and cognitive development.
♦ Attachment is a reciprocal relationship that occurs as a result of long-term interactions. First attachments occur in infancy between child and caregivers. They are characterized by mutual commitment and intense feelings. It is necessary for children to establish such attachments for subsequent mental health.
♦ Separation produces the responses of protest, despair and emotional detachment.
♦ Loss of attachment objects is distressing. The intensity of the grief is related to the degree of attachment.
♦ Bowlby proposed a four phase model of grief.
♦ Parkes proposed that loss causes psychosocial transitions because it challenges the assumptive world. He emphasized the cognitive-emotional processing required during grieving.
♦ Marris regarded grief as a process of psychological reintegration of the memory of the deceased.

Further reading

Bowlby, J. (1980) *Attachment and Loss, Vol. 3: Loss – Sadness and Depression.* London: The Hogarth Press.
Marris, P. (1986) *Loss and Change*, 2nd edn. London: Routledge.
Parkes, C.M. (1993) Bereavement as a psychosocial transition: processes of adaptation to change, in M.S. Stroebe, W. Stroebe, and R.O. Hansson (eds) *Handbook of Bereavement.* Cambridge: Cambridge University Press.
Parkes, C.M. (1996) *Bereavement*, 3rd edn. London: Routledge.

The development of models of adaptation to loss

In this chapter we introduce and discuss key conceptual models of loss and grief that have been developed over the last 30 years. The most widely used models describe grief as following a general pattern that may be subdivided into stages or phases. This approach is derived from the theoretical perspectives described in Chapter 4 (notably the work of Bowlby), augmented by clinical experience and empirical research, and has been referred to as the 'grief work' hypothesis. As mentioned in Chapter 4, this way of understanding grief has recently become the subject of critical debate. We outline this debate and introduce a number of refinements as well as new models that have been proposed.

Traditional models of grief: phases and stages

Lindemann (1944) was the first to propose that grief generally follows a recognizable pattern. His work has already been described in Chapter 4. Although Lindemann's sample was atypical in that he focused on people bereaved as a result of disaster, war or during psychiatric treatment, subsequent studies have generally confirmed his findings but also indicated that some experiences thought to be pathological, such as sensing the presence of the deceased, are now known to be relatively common (e.g. Parkes 1965b; Clayton 1974; Glick *et al.* 1974; Bowlby 1980). In Chapter 2, we described many of these manifestations and the interrelationship between physical and psychological responses. The impact of bereavement is complex and multidimensional and may affect emotions, cognitions, behaviour, physical health and social relationships. Bereaved people do not necessarily experience all the manifestations of grief, nor are those manifestations experienced at the same time. However, many contributors to the field have observed that there are common clusters of reactions that may typify certain time periods. Subsequently, phase and stage models have been developed to describe the usual course of grief (e.g. Averill 1968; Bowlby and Parkes 1970; Parkes 1972, 1986, 1996; DeVaul *et al.* 1979; Bowlby 1980; Marris 1986). In addition, Kubler-Ross' (1969) stage model of the grief of terminally ill people is often applied to other loss situations such as bereavement (e.g. Kalish 1985). We refer to these models as 'phase models' hereafter. Bowlby's concepts of phases of grief were discussed in the previous chapter.

The number and duration of phases vary and may be named differently but are remarkably similar. These models may be summarized as follows.

Numbness

The initial reaction is shock and disbelief accompanied by feelings of unreality and a sense of functioning on 'automatic pilot'. This may last from just a few hours to several days although, in our experience, bereaved people may describe themselves as 'feeling shocked' for a much longer period, even if the loss was anticipated. The sense of unreality may be interrupted by outbursts of anger or despair and feelings of anxiety and tension. Accompanying somatic symptoms may be evident.

Yearning

Gradually the numbness is replaced by the 'pangs of grief' – episodes of intense pining interspersed with periods of anxiety, tension, anger and self-reproach. The desire to recover what has been lost is intense and may be characterized by restless searching, vivid dreams, auditory and sensory awareness of the deceased and a preoccupation with memories. Crying aloud and sobbing is common, as is the suppression of emotions although anguish may be displayed in facial expressions of grief and deep sighing respirations (Parkes 1996: 45). The events leading up to the death may be obsessively reviewed and self-reproach is often associated with what has happened during this period. A wide range of conflicting feelings may be experienced such as agitation and lethargy. Physical symptoms include somatic distress, sleep disturbance and loss of appetite.

Despair

As the permanence of the loss is recognized, the intensity and frequency of the pangs of grief diminish and are replaced by despair and apathy. Expressions of these include social withdrawal and an inability to concentrate or to see anything worthwhile in the future. Somatic symptoms persist.

Recovery

Adapting to life without the deceased may take great effort, including rebuilding identity and purpose in life and acquiring new skills. Gradually people manage these adjustments more effectively and despair becomes interspersed with more positive feelings. Energy levels improve allowing new interests and relationships to be developed. However, even after years, people may report experiencing a pang of grief, usually triggered by specific events such as anniversaries, birthdays and family weddings. Similarly, hearing a special song, visiting a personally significant place or finding a treasured object may also cause grief to surface. These pangs are usually not as acute or as long-lasting as those experienced in the immediate aftermath of loss. The overall consensus is that grief is a long-term process and that it usually takes one to two years for the pangs of grief to become relatively self-contained and for social functioning to be restored, although it may take much longer. Some may come to feel that they have changed in positive ways (such as discovering inner strength) as a result of coping with their loss. Some would also argue that they have been irrevocably changed as a result of the loss, and that the term 'recovery' is inappropriate, as they will never be the same again.

Bowlby (1980: 93) firmly believed that working through the phases of grief was a necessary aspect of successful mourning:

> For mourning to have a favourable outcome it appears to be necessary for a bereaved person to endure this buffeting of emotion. Only if he [sic] can tolerate the pining, the more or less conscious searching, the seemingly endless examination of how and why the loss occurred, and the anger at anyone who might have been responsible, not sparing even the dead person, can he come gradually to recognise and accept that the loss is in truth permanent and that his life must be shaped anew.

Kubler-Ross (1969) developed a five stage model of the grief of terminally ill people that is often applied to grief following bereavement. Her model is derived from her clinical work as a psychiatrist, and the stages are described below.

Denial and isolation

As in other phase models, the initial reaction is denial, a natural coping mechanism that helps people manage their shock and take in the news. Another way in which patients may control their reactions is to not acknowledge the emotional impact while maintaining a cognitive understanding of their situation.

Anger

Once the truth of the diagnosis begins to be accepted, terminally ill people become angry. This anger may be intense and may be expressed in many ways; it may be directed towards the doctors and nurses providing care, towards family and friends, God, society in general or turned inward on the self.

Bargaining

When their anger has been expressed, terminally ill people attempt to bargain, often with God, in order to negotiate a cure, more time or greater relief from symptoms. For example, they may secretly promise to attend church regularly or become better people in return for being cured.

Depression

When bargaining does not work, the truth of impending death becomes more and more real and leads to depression. The feelings of sadness and loss may be overwhelming and accompanied by self-blame.

Acceptance

In this final stage, terminally ill people come to accept the reality of their death. They may become peaceful as they accept the inevitable. As their energy declines, they become less interested in their surroundings and those close to them. This withdrawal may be experienced as rejection and may be hard to understand if family and friends are not ready to let go of the patient.

According to Kubler-Ross (1969) not everyone will progress through all five stages, or experience them in the same order. Indeed, it may be hard for those working with dying patients to differentiate between denial and acceptance (Fitchett 1980) and in reality people may oscillate between both these states of consciousness.

Whereas Kubler-Ross may be criticized for being too simplistic, focusing on the experiences of relatively young people and those who die in hospital, her work has had a profound impact. By illustrating the isolation of terminal illness she has challenged the practice of protecting people by surrounding them with conspiracies of silence. However, her model is rather simplistic and there is a danger that those working with the dying may assume that they know how people are reacting and respond accordingly. As Frank (1991) points out, people may be reassured by knowing that others go through similar experiences but their feelings are personal and specific and not just a 'stage'. There is a danger that, rather than being enabled to explore their situation, dying people may find that their reactions are dismissed because they are recognized as 'normal'. Individual reactions that do not conform to the model may be ignored. As our main concern in this book is loss following bereavement, we will not discuss Kubler-Ross' model further, however, we would suggest that interested readers turn to Walter (1994: 70–8).

Parkes and Bowlby have had a major influence on the development of phase models of loss following bereavement. Parkes was inspired by

Bowlby's work on attachment and, as is made clear by Parkes (1996: 30), the two psychiatrists worked closely together to formulate their ideas (e.g. Bowlby and Parkes 1970). As has been described in Chapter 4, Parkes was also influenced by stress theory. In addition he drew on a programme of empirical research which included the following key studies: atypical reactions displayed by 21 bereaved adults attending the Bethlem Royal and Maudsley hospital in London (Parkes 1965a); the experiences of 22 younger (under 65 years) London widows (Parkes 1970); and the Harvard Bereavement Study, a longitudinal study of the experiences of 68 young widows and widowers (under 45 years) in the USA (Parkes and Brown 1972; Parkes and Weiss 1983).

Parkes' understanding of the 'normal' phases of grief has changed somewhat through the three editions of his major book *Bereavement: Studies of Grief in Adult Life* (Parkes 1972, 1986, 1996). The ideas expressed in the first edition have had a major impact on the understanding of grief. Parkes proposed a linear progression over time, although he recognized that grief reactions vary and that not everyone progresses at the same rate or experiences all the phases. Indeed, models generally conceptualize the phases of grief as fluid and overlapping (Kubler-Ross 1969; Parkes 1972, 1986). As Parkes (1986: 27) explains: '. . . grief is a process and not a state. Grief is not a set of symptoms which start after a loss and then gradually fade away. It involves a succession of clinical pictures which blend into and replace one another'. Parkes focused on the emotional and intra-psychic responses to loss. He emphasized the prevalence of anxiety, searching behaviour, anger and guilt and the necessity of working through these feelings in order to adapt to loss.

Worden (1982, 1991) refined the phases of grief. He proposed that, as grief is a process and not a state, people need to work through their reactions in order to make a complete adjustment. His model, the 'tasks of mourning' has been extremely influential and is widely used by those working with bereaved people. Worden drew on Freud's concept of grief work, Bowlby's attachment theory, developmental psychology and Engel's concept of grief as an illness. Engel (1961) argued that the psychological trauma of a major bereavement was analogous to the physiological trauma of a severe injury with mourning being necessary for successful healing. Consequently, if mourning is resisted it may remain incomplete, analogous to the partial healing of a wound.

Worden conceptualizes grief work as consisting of four overlapping tasks (see Table 5.1): bereaved people need to accept the death both intellectually and emotionally; they need to work through the emotional pain of loss while simultaneously adjusting to changes in circumstances, roles, status and identity; and they need to integrate the loss and let go of their emotional attachment to the deceased, so that they can invest in the present and the future (Worden 1982, 1991). Thus Worden's model places more emphasis on the cognitive, social and behavioural aspects of grief than earlier phase models.

Table 5.1 The tasks of mourning

Task	Description
Accept the reality of the loss	Intellectual and emotional acceptance of the loss
Work through the pain of grief	Experience the painful feelings
Adjust to the environment without the deceased	Adjust to changes in circumstance, role, identity, self-esteem and personal beliefs
Emotionally relocate the deceased and move on with life	Find a place for the deceased, let go of the emotional attachment and invest in new relationships

Source: Worden (1982, 1991).

Implicit in his approach is the belief that mourning can be influenced by intervention aimed at encouraging people to work through their grief.

As in previous phase models, Worden's tasks were not envisaged as following a specified progression although some ordering is implied in the definitions.

Task 1: to accept the reality of the loss

The first task is to accept that the deceased has gone and will not return; re-union is impossible. This task incorporates the searching behaviour described by Parkes and Bowlby. Worden describes three ways in which people may resist accepting the reality: they may deny the facts of the loss; deny the meaning of the loss; or they may deny that death is irreversible. Worden emphasizes that it is common for people to hope for reunion or assume that the deceased has not gone but that this illusion is usually short-lived, leading to task 2.

Task 2: to work through the pain of grief

Worden agrees with Parkes and Bowlby that suppressing the pain of grief prolongs mourning and that, although the intensity may vary, it is impossible to lose without experiencing pain. Drawing on Gorer (1965), Worden argues that expressing the pain of loss is more difficult in cultures that are uncomfortable with the expression of feelings. Thus, modern western cultures do not help people undertake task 2. The stigma that surrounds grief may cause mourners to believe that they should not need to grieve and encourage others to distract them. Some may seek to escape the pain of loss by cutting off from their feelings, avoiding painful thoughts, idealizing the dead or travelling in order to leave painful reminders behind.

Task 3: to adjust to the environment without the deceased

This depends on the relationship with the deceased and the various roles the deceased played. It involves developing new skills in order to manage new experiences such as facing an empty house and living alone, raising children alone, managing finances, etc. The degree to which the mourner's identity is dependent on their relationship with the deceased is also important. Women who define themselves through their role as wife may have to deal with a major loss of identity. Drawing on Horowitz *et al.* (1984), Worden argues that bereaved people may feel helpless, inadequate and incapable, especially if attempts to fulfil the deceased's roles fail. This may further lower self-esteem and challenge beliefs in personal efficacy. Like Parkes, Worden recognizes that loss has an impact on values, philosophical beliefs and assumptions and may lead to feelings of a loss of direction or purpose in life. As the loss becomes integrated new skills are developed and new beliefs adopted. However, some people may avoid completing task 3 by believing in their own helplessness or by withdrawing from the world.

Task 4: to emotionally relocate the deceased and move on with life

Worden bases task 4 on Freud's concept of the need for detachment. Originally he described the focus of this task as the need to withdraw emotional energy from the deceased and to reinvest it in another relationship. However, in the second edition of his book, Worden revised this task because he believed it had been misunderstood (Worden 1991: 16). He argues that bereaved people do not need to give up the deceased but rather to find an 'appropriate place' for them in their emotional lives, one that allows the deceased to continue to be important but that enables the mourner to carry on living effectively. Completing task 4 may be hindered by holding onto the past attachment so that life stops moving forward.

Complicated grief

Distortions, exaggerations or deviations from the 'normal' grief process proposed by phase models are described as 'abnormal' (e.g. Worden 1982, 1991) or 'pathological' grief (e.g. Parkes and Weiss 1983; Raphael 1984; Stroebe and Stroebe 1987; Parkes 1990) and people whose well-being continues to be impaired beyond the first year after bereavement are often referred to as having a 'poor outcome' (e.g. Sanders 1988). These terms have negative connotations, implying failure to grieve in the correct way. We prefer to describe grief as 'uncomplicated' or 'complicated'.

Complicated grief is conceptualized as, on the one hand, encompassing excessive intensity and prolonged duration and, on the other, absence of reaction and short duration. Thus the need to grieve may either be absent (Deutsch 1937; Bowlby 1980) or delayed (Lindemann 1944; Parkes 1965a), or chronic, and fail to resolve (Parkes 1965b; Shuchter and Zisook 1993). Phase models propose that if grief is initially absent it will either be manifested in some other way or appear at a later date. According to Bowlby (1980), sooner or later people who avoid all conscious grieving often break down, usually with some form of depression. According to this approach, absence of grief indicates avoidance which can only provide temporary relief from suffering as the necessity to mourn persists. Thus when grief is delayed, an initial apparent acceptance of the loss is followed some time later either by the onset of uncomplicated, or by chronic patterns of grief (Parkes 1970). During the delay, grief is either absent or 'distorted' – for example, there may be little sense of loss but over-activity, social withdrawal, physical illnesses or clinical depression. When grief is chronic, the usual manifestations are exaggerated and do not diminish over time.

Parkes and Weiss (1983) further describe complicated grief as unexpected, ambivalent or chronic syndromes arising from the circumstances of the death or the nature of the relationship with the deceased. For example, after the loss of an ambivalent relationship the initial reaction is one of relief followed by pining and despair and, as the opportunity to make amends has been lost, guilt. Parkes and Weiss regard the unexpected and ambivalent syndromes as being the prime cause of delayed grief and associate the chronic grief syndrome with highly dependent relationships. Their analysis suggests that different types of intervention may be more appropriate for different patterns of complicated mourning. However, their conclusions must be treated with some caution; their sample was atypical (aged under 46 years) and the sub-sample classified as having a 'bad' outcome was small (n=23). Further study is needed to confirm their hypotheses about the etiology of complicated grief.

The incidence of complicated grief is unclear. One problem is that complicated grief has not been consistently defined. Empirical studies, estimations of complicated grief and studies of the efficacy of interventions use health measures to assess outcomes rather than the concepts outlined above. Estimations vary, depending on which health measures are used, ranging from 5 per cent (Clayton 1982), to 17 per cent (Zisook and DeVaul 1985) to around a third of bereaved people showing little adaptation by the end of the first year (Raphael 1984; Kessler et al. 1985; Stroebe et al. 1988; Cleiren 1991). Moreover, empirical studies have revealed the individuality of mourning, making it harder to draw clear distinctions between uncomplicated and complicated reactions (Middleton et al. 1993; Shuchter and Zisook 1993). Many of Lindemann's (1944) symptoms of distorted grief, for example, are now recognized as common experiences. Clearly, definitions of complicated grief should be applied with care and hasty judgements should be avoided. Indeed, models of grief may need to be much more flexible than that proposed by the traditional models outlined above.

Criticisms of phase models and the grief work hypothesis

In this section we review recent criticisms of phase models and the 'grief work hypothesis' which is central to this view of grieving. Stroebe (1992/3: 19–20) sums up this approach as follows:

Generally speaking, 'grief work' implies a cognitive process of confronting a loss, of going over events before and at the time of death, of focusing on memories and working towards detachment from the deceased. It requires an active, ongoing, effortful attempt to come to terms with loss. Fundamental to current conceptions is the view that one needs to bring the reality of loss into one's awareness as much as possible and that suppression is a pathological phenomenon.

Wortman and Silver (1989) argue that this constitutes the 'clinical lore' of coping with loss. Indeed, there is evidence that many bereaved people and professionals believe that it is an incontestable fact that grief proceeds in stages (Wambach 1985) and many accounts of bereavement counselling focus on the necessity of helping people to express their feelings and work through grief (e.g. Lendrum and Syme 1992). Thus, phase models have had a powerful influence in defining normality for both lay people and professionals. However, a number of important criticisms have been made. These question the way in which phase models have been interpreted clinically and the empirical base for the necessity of grief work.

Phase models may be misinterpreted and used prescriptively

Even though accounts of phase models have always stressed the interweaving of phases, there has been a tendency for them to be interpreted as linear, normative prescriptions of how bereaved people should respond (Osterweis *et al.* 1984; Wortman and Silver 1989). This can be misleading as there is ample evidence that (as recognized in the original texts) expressions of grief, the timing and sequence of phases, the duration of mourning and general coping responses vary (see Stroebe *et al.* 1993b). If phase models are used prescriptively, diversity may be denied and hasty judgements made about whether grief is 'normal' or 'abnormal'. One personal account of bereavement counselling describes being on the receiving end of the prescriptive use of the phases of grief. Ellmann (1994) describes how she was offered six one-hour sessions to work through three stages of bereavement: two for denial, two for guilt and two for anger. Ellmann concluded that her counsellor wanted her grief to be 'packaged and frozen' and made safe and consequently felt that the counsellor could not engage with the rawness of her feelings. Indeed, grief may be too complex and variable to be encompassed by phase models. For example, Shuchter and Zisook point out that their empirical research led them to the conclusion that the grief process is so individualized and variable, and involves so many different facets of the bereaved person that 'attempts to limit its scope or demarcate its boundaries by arbitrarily defining normal grief are bound to fail' (Shuchter and Zisook 1993: 23).

In addition, Kubler-Ross' (1969) stage theory of the grief of terminally ill people is often misinterpreted and applied to bereavement (e.g. Kalish 1985). Whereas the initial impact of a terminal diagnosis and the death of a loved one may be similar in some respects, the grief trajectory may be different. In the former, the terminally ill person grieves for the lack of a future and for a life being cut short. In the latter, the bereaved person mourns the loss of the deceased and the life shared with them. For example, Kubler-Ross' stage of bargaining is not mentioned by other grief models and, as we discuss later in this chapter, the concept of letting go has been widely challenged.

Difficulties with the grief work hypothesis

Wortman and Silver (1989) have identified a number of important criticisms about the assumptions associated with the notion of 'grief work'.

Distress or depression is inevitable

The grief work hypothesis assumes that everyone who experiences a loss will be distressed. However, studies of bereaved people show that levels of distress, and the proportion who become depressed, vary. According to Parkes (1996), Wortman and Silver (1989) have confused distress with clinical depression. He argues that while depression is not inevitable, distress is, and he cites anthropological evidence to support this claim. In many different cultures people show some signs of grieving, although the expression of grief is very variable. He considers that only people who have no attachment to the deceased would show no reaction to the loss, a conclusion that is supported by Silverman (1986) in her study of widows.

Distress is necessary and grief must be 'worked through'

The notion of grief work assumes that people need to confront the pain of loss in order to reach a successful resolution. As described earlier, distress is assumed to be necessary and not showing distress is thought to be an important indicator of complicated grief. However, there is evidence that those who are most distressed in the early weeks of bereavement are those who are more likely to continue to be distressed in the long term (Vachon et al. 1982b; Parkes and Weiss 1983). According to Wortman and Silver (1989), this indicates that grief work may be problematic. For example, Parkes and Weiss' (1983) high initial distress, high yearning group, though small, followed a chronic grief pattern. Is high distress symptomatic of grief work or may it reflect other factors such as the age of the respondents (under 45) or a lack of support? To what extent is Wortman and Silver's argument diminished because it is supported by reference to groups of people whose grief was complicated?

Similarly, Wortman and Silver (1989) confuse low distress and absence of grief in order to argue that 'working through' grief may not be necessary. Low distress (rather than the absence of distress) has been found to be an indicator of resilience and a failure to express emotion does not necessarily result in a poor outcome (Vachon et al. 1982a; Parkes and Weiss 1983). Indeed, bereaved people may experience high levels of stress while drawing on personal strength, resourcefulness and resilience. Lund et al. (1993) emphasize the resilience of bereaved people. They found that while widow(er)s may feel angry, guilty and lonely, they may simultaneously feel a sense of personal strength and pride in the way they are coping. While the majority experienced bereavement as the most stressful event that they had encountered, and reported quite high levels of stress, they also reported numerous indicators of personal strength, resourcefulness and resilience. The fact that most were Mormons may have influenced their results, as many reported finding personal strengths that they had previously been unaware of, and coped better than expected.

The expectation of recovery

Phase models assume that the final outcome of grieving will be a return to normal psychological and social functioning. Wortman and Silver (1989) provide a more convincing argument for revising this concept of 'recovery' suggesting that, for a minority of individuals, grieving may continue for many years without it becoming complicated. Few studies have followed people for more than two years so it is difficult to know how long 'normal' grief should last. In addition, it may be argued that loss changes people such that they are never the same again, although this does not mean that they are psychologically damaged. Indeed, as described above there is evidence that they may become more aware of their resourcefulness.

Further evidence for revising the concept of recovery is provided by Klass et al. (1996). In their book *Continuing Bonds*, a number of studies are presented, notably of bereaved parents and grieving children, that suggest that the deceased may continue to influence the lives of bereaved people without problems occurring. Klass et al. argue that Freud (1917), Bowlby (1980) and Parkes (1972, 1986) all observed this phenomenon but explained these data in terms of their existing theoretical frameworks. In sum, a convincing body of empirical research now bears out Marris' (1986) conclusions about the continuing importance of the meaning of the relationship with the deceased. These may include memories, identifying with the deceased, incorporating their ideas and continuing their work (Shuchter and Zisook 1993). Grief may not, therefore, have a definite end point which marks recovery. People may adapt to new roles and regain their interest in life but as Silverman points out, in doing so 'People don't give up the past, they change their relationship to it' (1986: 7).

Rather than letting go, bereaved people negotiate and renegotiate the meaning of the loss, constructing new connections with the deceased. Over time the manifestations of grief do become less intense and less frequent with a gradual change in orientation toward the future, but the deceased continue to play a role in the reality of the living. Relationships with others inform who we are and their importance, meaning and influence are not severed by loss.

Limitations of empirical studies

The research base was limited when the models of grief were developed. However, phase models were influenced by a number of empirical studies. For an extensive review of these studies interested readers should refer to Stroebe and Stroebe (1987). Many studies focused on bereavement and health and, while laying a foundation for future research, many issues remain unresolved due to a number of methodological limitations.

Dominance of widows

Models and theories of bereavement were developed to explain the process of conjugal loss and influential studies have focused on the experiences of young, white, middle-class widows (Hockey 1997). Consequently, models and theories of grief may be gynocentric, reflecting women's experience of the loss of a spouse. Gender may influence coping styles (as we discuss further later) and, as described above, recent studies, particularly of grieving children or adults who have lost a child, suggest that the explanations provided by phase models may be somewhat limited.

Age cohort effect

The studies that informed the development of the grief work hypothesis and phase models were undertaken in the 1970s or earlier and may reflect social norms that no longer hold true. For example, the widows described by Parkes (1972, 1986, 1993b) may be described as having stereotypical relationships with their husbands, deriving their sense of self primarily from their relationship as wife. Torrie (1987) describes the problems of widows using Cruse Bereavement Care in the 1960s and 1970s as predominantly the consequence of living in a male orientated society where women were economically dependent on their husbands, and when widowed they often became second-class citizens with little status. Women's roles have changed dramatically in recent years and these changes may influence their response to loss and its impact on health and well-being.

Ethnicity

Models of grief are based on empirical studies and clinical practice under-taken in modern western societies, notably the USA, Australia and the UK. Even within these countries, studies have failed to recognize ethnic differences. Furthermore, the majority of contributors to recent major books on bereavement (e.g. Stroebe *et al.* 1993a; Klass *et al.* 1996) work in North America and it must not be assumed that their findings will hold true, even for other western societies. As described in Chapter 1 cultures differ widely in defining what is considered to be an appropriate expression of grief. There is a need for cross-cultural research to test the applicability of findings and to test popular views, such as the belief that grief is resolved more rapidly and with less risk to well-being when people continue to follow traditional mourning rituals. The literature has recently begun to acknowledge the notion that ethnicity has important implications for the course of grief (e.g. Field *et al.* 1997; Parkes *et al.* 1997).

High refusal rates

These are the norm for studies of bereavement, which rarely exceed 60 per cent acceptance rates. Empirical studies tend to suffer from small sample sizes and the consequent problems such as volunteer effects. For example, those who refuse have been found to be more upset (Caserta and Lund 1992) or have more problems (Cleiren 1991) than those who participate. Stroebe *et al.* (1988) experienced a very high refusal rate in their study of 60 matched widows and widowers. This reflected a gender bias; widows who refused were less depressed than those who participated while the opposite was true for widowers.

Lack of control groups

The impact of grief can only be demonstrated by comparing bereaved and non-bereaved people. However, many studies do not include non-bereaved control groups and this has led to some false assumptions about the effects of bereavement. The greater symptomatology of widows compared to widowers, for example, led some researchers to conclude that women are more vulnerable than men. When widows and widowers are compared to matched married controls it becomes apparent that the former conclusion reflected the main effects of gender on health and, in fact, the impact of bereavement is more pronounced for men (Stroebe and Stroebe 1983).

Lack of reliable measures of grief

There is a lack of agreement on what constitutes adequate measures of outcome. The changing symptomatology of grief over time makes it difficult to generate reliable measures to assess and classify the manifestations of grief and provide criteria for recovery. Measures of adjustment have included a reduction in depressive symptoms, returning to a 'usual' level of social functioning, remarriage, reduction in frequency of distressing memories and the capacity to form new relationships and undertake new social roles. Not only are these difficult to measure, some, such as remarriage, are too gross. The validity and reliability of measures used in the studies that informed the development of phase models, such as the health questionnaire used in the Harvard Bereavement Study (Parkes and Brown 1972; Glick et al. 1974; Parkes and Weiss 1983) was not well established as the field was relatively unexplored. Later instruments such as the grief experience inventory (Sanders et al. 1985) and the Texas Revised Inventory of Grief (Faschingbauer et al. 1987) have adequate reliability but have not been tested in the UK.

Self-report

Data collection in many studies of bereavement relies on self-report with no comparative pre-loss measures. Bereaved people may either exaggerate or under-report the effects of loss in order to comply with social expectations. Respondents may feel that admitting to well-being may be taken as an indication of lack of love for the deceased or, conversely, that they are expected to be coping well and therefore minimize their distress. The latter is particularly likely to hold for men (Berardo 1970).

To summarize, the grief work hypothesis and the phase models of grief do not adequately account for the diversity of grief suggested by recent empirical studies of wider populations. However, it must be emphasized that the original work attempted to describe common grief experiences rather than to be prescriptive. It is extremely difficult to capture multidimensional, complex human processes in a model that is simple to use, and we must question whether this is feasible or possible. Wortman and Silver (1989) concluded that there are three patterns of grief. Bereaved people may move from high distress to low distress and conform to the expected pattern, may never experience high distress or may continue to be distressed for years. Nevertheless the general consensus is that phase models provide useful general descriptions of the course of grief and can be of great value as a general guide for both professionals and lay people, helping them to understand common grief experiences. However, they may need to be augmented by other models.

New models of grief

A number of new models of grief have been developed to account for the limitations of phase models.

The multidimensional model

Le Poidevin refined the phases of grief by developing a multidimensional model while working at St Christopher's Hospice with Parkes in the early 1980s (see Parkes *et al.* 1996). She aimed to develop a model that would enable those working with bereaved people to understand the individual context of grief within the wider frameworks provided by the phase and task approaches. She conceptualized grief as a process of simultaneous change along seven dimensions, including the social, behavioural and spiritual dimensions of grief as well as the emotional and physical. Although widely used by counsellors who attended Le Poidevin's training courses on bereavement, her model remained unpublished at her untimely death in 1989. By describing the main areas of life that are affected by loss, the dimensions of loss enable those offering support or counselling to gain an understanding of the individual and their grief reactions. The model helps us to understand the person's circumstances, what problems they are facing and, importantly,

Table 5.2   The dimensions of loss

Dimension	Description
Emotional: strong emotions are usual	How comfortable is the individual with their emotional responses? Do they believe in emotional control or are they at ease with expressing feelings?
Social: loss is experienced within a social network; it may cause changes in status and in role	What has been the impact on other members of the social network? What quality of support is available? What changes in status or role have to be negotiated?
Physical: physical symptoms are common	What has been the impact on physical health?
Lifestyle: loss may lead to major changes in lifestyle such as having to move house or cope with financial difficulties	Has loss caused changes in lifestyle?
Practical: loss may affect the ability to cope with the practicalities of everyday life such as cooking, shopping, self-care, child care and housework	How are everyday practicalities being managed?
Spiritual: loss may cause people to question their beliefs about the world and lead to a loss of meaning and purpose	In what ways has bereavement affected religious or other spiritual belief systems? What meaning has been ascribed to the loss?
Identity: loss may affect identity, self-esteem and feelings of self-worth	To what extent has loss affected the individual's self-concept and self-esteem?

what resources are available to help them cope. Table 5.2 outlines the dimensions and the main areas of concern for those providing loss intervention. The clinical use of this model is described in Chapter 6.

Following a longitudinal study of 350 widows and widowers in San Diego, Shuchter and Zisook (1993) also proposed that a multidimensional model of grief helps to prevent grief from being viewed as a static or linear process. Like Le Poidevin they stress the value of a model that underlines the individuality of reactions, and outline six dimensions:

1 emotional and cognitive responses;
2 coping with emotional pain;
3 the continuing relationship with the dead spouse;
4 changes in functioning;
5 changes in relationships;
6 changes in identity.

The dual process model (DPM)

A recent and significant advance in our understanding of grief is provided by the DPM developed by Stroebe and Schut (1996). It is derived from a careful examination of empirical research which brought them to conclude that avoiding grief may be both helpful and detrimental. Their framework draws on traditional models but introduces a new concept – that of oscillation between coping behaviours.

Stroebe and Schut argue that there are two aspects involved in adapting to bereavement: loss orientation and restoration orientation. Loss orientation encompasses grief work, including being preoccupied with the loss, ruminating and yearning for the deceased and associated behaviours such as visiting places or listening to music that will trigger sorrow. Restoration orientation encompasses mastering the tasks and roles undertaken by the deceased, making lifestyle adjustments, coping with everyday life, building a new identity and seeking distractions from painful thoughts. Stroebe and Schut believe that it is important for bereaved people to take time off from the emotions of grief that otherwise would be too overwhelming. This enables them to manage daily life and all the changes that are secondary to bereavement and that also trigger anxiety and further feelings of loss. Building on Worden (1982, 1991), they developed four restoration-oriented tasks:

1 to take time off from the pain of grief;
2 to master the subjective environment in which the deceased is missing;
3 to develop new roles and relationships;
4 to accept the reality of the changed world.

Central to this analysis is the concept of oscillation between loss- and restoration-focused behaviour. Both are necessary for adjustment, although the degree and emphasis on each approach will vary for each individual depending on the circumstances of their loss, personality factors, gender and cultural background. Thus, some men may cope by being more oriented toward restoration whereas some women may adopt a more loss-oriented style of coping. Neither orientation is gender specific; it is a matter of degree or emphasis. Similarly, some cultures may emphasize one type of behaviour over another. In the broader context, behaviour is likely to shift over time from loss orientation towards restoration. Complicated grief is accounted for by extremes of behaviour; unremitting confrontation or avoidance are associated with chronic or absent grief and poor adaptation.

As Stokes *et al.* (1997) observe, bereaved people may oscillate between restoration and loss on a daily basis as well as over time. Whether a client is in restoration or loss mode will influence their responses to others, including those seeking to offer support or counselling. Rather than suggesting that the focus must be on loss, the DPM recognizes that both expressing and controlling feelings are important. It affirms the importance of addressing the secondary stresses of bereavement summarized by Worden's (1991) third task of mourning. It suggests that supporting ways of coping and the resilience of the mourner is as important as addressing their emotional responses. The model implies that judgements about the way a bereaved person is coping should not be made too quickly. However, the model remains to be tested and the degree of oscillation necessary for effective grieving remains open. It may be criticized for continuing to place greater emphasis on the psychology of grieving rather than the social context of bereavement. In particular the DPM does not explain the role of interpersonal relationships in helping people cope with loss. Nevertheless it provides a useful addition to existing models of grief.

Biographical models

As noted earlier, a convincing body of empirical research supports the continuing importance of the relationship with the deceased. Walter's (1996a) biographical model of grief emphasizes the importance of talking to others about the deceased. He argues that conversations with others help bereaved people to construct a durable biography that enables them to integrate the relationship into their ongoing lives (Walter 1996a: 7). The importance of talking to others is not to work through distress but to discover the meaning of the relationship, echoing Marris' (1986) theory of grief described in Chapter 4. According to Walter (1996a), biography construction is best achieved by talking to others who knew the deceased. He suggests that bereavement counsellors are a poor second best as they cannot engage in the reality testing that is an important part of creating an accurate biography. However, Walter's understanding of the role of bereavement counsellors is narrow, illustrated by his highly selective reading of Lendrum and Syme (1992). His conclusions provide a salutary reminder of the lack of evaluation of the effectiveness of bereavement services. He suggests that bereavement counsellors discourage people from talking about the deceased by focusing exclusively on emotions, although in a more recent paper (Walter 1997b) he acknowledged the useful role that counsellors may play.

Walter's analysis is derived from Giddens' theory of the social construction of identity (Giddens 1991). Social change has led to an increased detachment from tradition, place, kinship, religion and fixed roles. Consequently people need to continuously construct and reconstruct their identity and this is achieved primarily through discourse with others. The impact of social change, with an ageing population and increasing geographical mobility, means that bereaved people have become less likely to have access to others who both knew and are willing to talk about the deceased. They may have lost the person with whom they interacted most frequently, others may not be available, may lose patience with the bereaved person's way of mourning or hold conflicting views of the deceased. It may be difficult, therefore, to jointly construct a biography. It must be recognized that interpersonal processes may both facilitate and impede intra-psychic change following bereavement. Thus, while attacking the focus of bereavement counselling as being misguided, Walter clearly presents the value of talking to others acting as substitutes when social networks are inadequate.

Walter (1996a) suggests that the biographical model may be a male model as it is derived from his own experience of bereavement and describes a cognitive process. His model may be criticized because it has not been empirically tested and is derived from a very narrow perspective. His belief that working through emotions is not as important as constructing a biography may also represent the difference between his personal experience (the death on his elderly father and the loss of a friend) and the grief that accompanies the death of a long-term partner. Stroebe (1997), in a critical review of Walter's model, points out that regaining emotional equilibrium and integrating the meaning of the relationship are connected rather than separate processes. Moreover, Walter does not explain how interactions with others bring about change nor does he provide an adequate explanation for complicated grief or how social networks might enable the latter to be resolved. In sum, Walter's model does not replace previous theories but, by emphasizing the interpersonal, societal context of grief, it provides a useful supplement.

Conclusions

Traditionally, grief has been described as a time bounded process consisting of phases, stages or tasks. This perspective has great value but has been simplistically represented in textbooks on grief for both health care professionals and the lay public. New models have been developed to account for the individuality and diversity of grief and to encompass the social, behavioural and spiritual dimensions of loss as well as the psychological and physical. The DPM seems to be of particular value as it encompasses coping styles. It continues to be developed and tested by Stroebe, Schut and their colleagues at the University of Utrecht. The search to understand loss and its ramifications continues. Recent years have seen the development of more subtle, holistic accounts. However, given our growing understanding of the interplay between loss, coping, personality and social factors, it is likely that our models of grief will continue to be refined. Models may be used to guide research but a not inconsiderable test is their usefulness for intervention. In the next chapter we discuss how helpful models of grief are for those who seek to provide support and counselling to bereaved people.

Summary

♦ Bereavement has multiple consequences affecting psychological, physical and social well-being. It is associated with periods of acute emotional distress and secondary stress resulting from the process of adapting to changed life circumstances.

♦ Grief reactions were observed to cluster and models were developed to describe the process of uncomplicated grief over time. Traditional models included phases and stages of grief and the tasks of mourning and drew on theoretical perspectives that emphasized the need for grief work. Not undertaking or completing grief was thought to be problematic and to lead to grief becoming complicated.

♦ Traditional models of grief were not meant to be prescriptive but have commonly been viewed as such. They have been criticized for not accounting for the diversity and individuality of reactions and for neglecting resourcefulness. The grief work hypothesis has been criticized and evidence from empirical studies has challenged concepts of 'recovery'.

♦ In addition, early studies of bereavement that informed the traditional models suffer from a number of shortcomings particularly the dominance of young, white, middle-class widows.

♦ In sum, although there are many common features, grief varies both in intensity and in the extent to which it interferes with individual functioning. Grief cannot be plotted in a series of well-defined phases. Phase models of grief should be used as valuable general guides to understanding rather than as a prescriptive schema of uncomplicated and complicated grief.

♦ New models of grief have been developed. These include multidimensional models that enable understanding of the individuality of grief, the DPM that introduces the concept of oscillation between those coping behaviours that focus on the loss and those that focus on the future with both being important for adaptation, and biographical models that stress the importance of talking about the deceased in order to find meaning in the loss.

Further reading

Field, D., Hockey, J. and Small, N. (1997) *Death, Gender and Ethnicity*. London: Routledge.

Klass, D., Silverman, P.R. and Nickman, S.L. (1996) *Continuing Bonds*. Philadelphia: Taylor & Francis.

Parkes, C.M. (1996) *Bereavement: Studies of Grief in Adult Life*, 3rd edn. London: Routledge.

Stroebe, W. and Stroebe, M.S. (1987). *Bereavement and Health*. Cambridge: Cambridge University Press.

Stroebe, M.S., Stroebe, W. and Hansson, R.O. (eds) (1993) *Handbook of Bereavement: Theory, Research and Intervention*. Cambridge: Cambridge University Press.

Worden, J.W. (1991) *Grief Counselling and Grief Therapy*, 2nd edn. New York: Springer Publishing.

The application of models of loss in clinical and community settings

As discussed in Chapters 4 and 5, there is broad agreement that grief needs to be engaged with, and worked through, before mourners can regain their equilibrium and adapt to their new situation and status. Bereavement support programmes aim to facilitate the grief process and to help people cope with any difficulties in order to avoid long-term deleterious health consequences. In this chapter we discuss the theoretical base for providing bereavement services and how models of loss are used to guide interventions. We outline the different approaches that have been developed and raise key issues such as the need for bereavement counselling and the role of volunteers.

Offering this type of support makes demands on the individuals involved. How do they cope with their exposure to the distress and grief of others? We consider the concept of burnout and the possible strategies used to support bereavement workers.

The theoretical base of bereavement services

In Chapters 4 and 5 we described and discussed theories and models of grief and bereavement. We discussed the widely held view that people need to work through their grief in order to 'recover'. According to this model, grief is similar to an illness and intervention provides a 'cure' by helping people work through the phases or tasks of mourning. The work of Bowlby and Parkes has been important in the development of this model and attachment theory has had a profound influence both on our understanding of grief and on psychodynamic counselling. Indeed, attachment theory has been found to be the primary theoretical framework used by professional 'experts' working with bereaved people (Middleton *et al.* 1991). As we discussed in Chapter 5, the grief work model has been subject to criticism, both from a theoretical and from a clinical perspective. While phase and task models provide counsellors with a helpful description of the major themes of grief over time (from incomprehension, through distress to adaptation) they do not account for the diversity of grief. As discussed in Chapter 5, there is a danger that they may be used prescriptively and that supporters will try and make bereaved people fit the model of grief rather than trying to understand their individual context.

Viewing grief as a period of transition suggests that bereaved people may be helped in other ways. Parkes (1993b) argues that people in transition require both emotional support and assistance in discovering new models of the world appropriate to the emerging situation. Bereaved people need the support and understanding of others. Such support may help by encouraging them to talk about their situation and thereby review and relearn their inner assumptions about the world (Parkes 1993b), and to construct an enduring bond with the deceased (Klass *et al.* 1996). By providing support, helpers may become 'agents of change, midwives at the birth of new identities' (Parkes 1993b: 99). This approach acknowledges that bereaved people need support but that this may be provided by the social network, lay helpers and professionals without specialist training as well as highly trained counsellors and other mental health professionals.

According to stress and coping theory, bereavement will only be stressful (in addition to distressing), if the bereaved person's coping resources are inadequate. The *perception* that social support is inadequate is the best replicated risk factor associated with bereavement (Sanders 1993). According to stress theory, therefore, the aim of support is to compensate for deficits in social support and bolster the individual's resources in order to prevent, or ameliorate, the risks associated with bereavement. As described in Chapter 2, social support may mediate between stress and health and may have a positive effect on the immune system. It may directly influence well-being and enable individuals to cope, or it may provide a 'buffer' between the individual and the stressful event.

It is tempting, therefore, to assume that bereaved people who have family and friends nearby will not need formal bereavement care. However, it must be remembered that the relationship between social support and bereavement is dynamic. Bereavement may deprive people of a confidant and a prime source of emotional support, feedback and reassurance at a time of enormous change and anxiety. Geographical mobility means that bereaved people may live some distance from kin and close friends and changes in role and status may influence the availability of support, particularly among widows (Lopata 1975; Silverman 1986). Moreover, bereavement affects whole social networks, not just key carers and members may not have the emotional energy to help each other (Vachon and Stylianos 1988). There may be different patterns of grief and existing tensions may be exacerbated. Indeed, family discord is a common source of additional stress (Maddison and Walker 1967; Lopata 1979; Littlewood 1987). Machin (1996), for example, found that contact with kin was much lower than anticipated after bereavement and Cleiren (1991) reported that bereaved people often choose not to talk to relatives about their problems because they recognize that they are also grieving.

As described in Chapter 1, bereaved people remind others of the fact of mortality. This may cause potential supporters to feel anxious. Rather than causing further distress, they may choose to avoid the bereaved person, or subjects that may cause their grief to be expressed. Lehman *et al.* (1986), for example, found that bereaved people were much more likely to be offered advice than given the opportunity to express feelings and that those close to them were the least likely to be helpful. Lehman *et al.* concluded that there are inherent tensions in interactions with bereaved people that inhibit supportive behaviour. Moreover, displays of distress exacerbate the anxiety of potential supporters and angry or depressed people may alienate or exhaust supporters (Stroebe and Stroebe 1987).

According to Lattanzi (1982: 57), 'Most people find it difficult to be around grieving persons. Our own discomfort and feelings of helplessness lead us to patterns of avoiding people who are bereaved. Many of us would like to hurry along the grief process for individuals so that we can feel more at ease with them'.

In summary, rather than providing emotional support and buffering, social support systems may break under the strain of bereavement (Vachon and Stylianos 1988) leaving mourners further bereft and with many unmet needs (Machin 1996).

Possible factors contributing to lack of support for bereaved people

- Geographical mobility
- Loss of support provided by the deceased
- Impact of bereavement on social network
- Changes in role and status
- Anxiety experienced by others when interacting with bereaved people
- Personality factors

Stress and coping theory suggests that in general bereaved people are unlikely to need sophisticated therapy but rather support that compensates for the inadequacy of informal networks. Such support may be provided by volunteers or by people who have experienced bereavement themselves and wish to help others in similar situations. As Raphael (1980: 162) states: 'The background to all bereavement counselling is general support, support that offers human comfort and care that accepts and encourages appropriate grief and mourning'. Indeed, while many professionals work with bereaved people, volunteers play a major role in bereavement services in the UK.

Stress and coping theory also offers the rationale for providing pro-active services aimed at preventing problems arising. As discussed in Chapter 2, the majority of bereaved people do not experience long-term problems following bereavement. However, as many as one third of bereaved people may be at risk. It is this group who may benefit from support or counselling.

Although those in need of specialized professional services after bereavement are small in number, their need is great. There is increased risk of suicide after bereavement (Kaprio et al. 1987), increased risk of recurrence of previous psychiatric problems (Parkes 1972), and increased risk of serious depression (see Jacobs et al. 1989). These obviously serious outcomes are not the only causes for concern; there are also people who, while they may not fall into a clear diagnostic category, are disturbed and unhappy for years (sometimes for ever) after experiencing the death of someone close. The quality of their lives, and often the lives of those nearest to them, is much reduced, and they may become socially isolated because their mood and behaviour make them unrewarding or unpleasant to be with. They may also be vulnerable to the overuse of drugs such as alcohol and tobacco, with health-damaging consequences. A range of behaviours that might in other circumstances be described as disturbed is common after bereavement. In the acute stages of grief, as we have already discussed, motor restlessness, sleeplessness and agitation are common. They may be followed by a period of lethargy and apathy, sometimes accompanied by self-neglect, which characteristically resolves with time.

The identification of risk factors

The identification of risk factors associated with long-term difficulties following bereavement is important. It has been demonstrated that these can be used to assess risk and that, by providing ongoing support, the risks to health and well-being may be significantly reduced (Raphael 1977; Parkes 1981). This approach has been widely adopted by hospices following the pioneering role of the St Christopher's Hospice bereavement service (Parkes 1981) with support largely being offered by volunteers.

In recent years, in the wake of findings such as those of the Harvard Study (Parkes and Weiss 1983) and other work by Parkes, Raphael and others (summarized in Parkes 1986) there has been mounting evidence for the association of risk factors with poor outcome. The identification of risk factors permits at least the theoretical possibility of targetting certain bereaved people for prophylactic intervention.

The following factors have been shown to be associated with health deterioration following bereavement.

Age

There is conflicting evidence about the influence of age. As discussed earlier, epidemiological studies of mortality rates indicate that younger widowers are at risk. Other studies suggest that younger people experience more health problems (Maddison and Walker 1967; Clayton 1974; Ball 1977; Stroebe and Stroebe 1987). In contrast, Cleiren (1991) found that kinship and the quality of attachment were more important factors than age. He suggests that these may be masked in studies which focus exclusively on the widowed. Parkes (1972) suggests that 'timely' deaths are less distressing because they fit expectations. However, 'timeliness' may depend on relationship factors and complicated outcomes are not confined to the young. Older widow(er)s may suffer continuing psychological reactions that are distressing (Gallagher-Thompson *et al.* 1993).

Gender

Although women report more symptoms than men (Parkes and Brown 1972), comparisons of widowed and married people show that widowers are at greater risk (Young *et al.* 1963; Rees and Lutkins 1967; Parkes 1970; Helsing and Szklo 1981; Parkes and Weiss 1983; Stroebe and Stroebe 1983).

Relationship to the deceased

Most studies have focused on conjugal bereavement and, as discussed earlier, there is clear evidence that the loss of a spouse is detrimental to well-being. Other relationships have also been associated with an increased vulnerability including loss of an adult child (Cleiren 1991), being a sister of the deceased (Cleiren 1991), and bereavement in childhood (Brown and Harris 1978).

Nature of relationship to the deceased

Ambivalent (Parkes 1975; Parkes and Weiss 1983) and dependent relationships (Parkes 1975; Lopata 1979; Parkes and Weiss 1983; Raphael 1984; Bankoff 1986), and socially unacknowledged relationships, such as lovers or gay and lesbian partnerships, have been associated with problematic outcomes.

Personality

Although few studies have directly focused on personality factors there is some evidence that they influence the course of grief (Sanders 1988). They include: severe reactions to previous losses (Parkes 1986); low self-esteem (Parkes and Weiss 1983; Stroebe and Stroebe 1987: Lund *et al.* 1993); low trust of self (Parkes 1990); being more anxious and worrying (Sanders 1981; Vachon et al. 1982a; Parkes and Weiss 1983); a perceived lack of control (Stroebe et al. 1988; Cleiren 1991); and coping by denial of emotion or extreme self-reliance (Sanders 1981). Parkes describes intense clinging as characteristic of a 'grief prone personality' (Parkes and Weiss 1983). The importance of personality factors is controversial with some arguing that the prior neglect of this area has led to misinterpretation of research data (McCrae and Costa 1993). For example, characteristics of depressed widow(er)s, such as poor social support, may arise from personality traits rather than bereavement *per se* (Cleiren 1991). Thus some people attract warmth and compassion while others perceive hostility when none is intended and feel that their needs are not being met despite the good intentions of others. Personality measures indicative of resilience and good outcome include the ability to communicate feelings and thoughts to others, high personal esteem and personal competency (Lund et al. 1993).

Preexisting health

Poor physical and psychological health pre-bereavement is associated with poor adaptation (Parkes and Weiss 1983; Cleiren 1991). These may be exacerbated by the stress of bereavement.

Circumstances of the death

Such as protracted terminal illness, unexpected, untimely, violent or stigmatized deaths, for example, suicide (see Ball 1977; Parkes and Weiss 1983; Sanders 1983; Lundin 1984; Stroebe et al. 1988), or following a protracted terminal illness (Sanders 1983) such as cancer (Vachon et al. 1977). However, Cleiren's (1991) study, comparing bereavement after death from road traffic accidents, suicide or long-term illness found that the mode of death had no long-term impact on adaptation.

Concurrent crises

Individuals facing multiple crises and concurrent stress, such as other losses and low income, have been found to be at greater risk (Parkes 1975; Sanders 1988). Reductions in income and lowered socio-economic status are also detrimental (Glick et al. 1974; Parkes 1975; Lopata 1979; Vachon et al. 1982a).

Initial grief reactions

High initial distress is related to long-term health deterioration (Vachon et al. 1982a; Parkes and Weiss 1983) and poor social functioning (Cleiren 1991).

Social support

A perceived lack of social support has been associated with poor health outcomes in the first year after bereavement (Maddison and Walker 1967; Parkes 1970; Bunch 1972; Parkes and Weiss 1983), continued high distress two years after bereavement (Vachon *et al.* 1982a; Parkes and Weiss 1983) and difficulties in role adjustment (Bankoff 1986).

Risk factors fall into three groups: social, personal (e.g. personality characteristics, health) and circumstantial (e.g. mode of death and concurrent crises). The relative strength of individual risk factors is unclear. For example, Stroebe *et al.* (1988) found that a perceived lack of internal control over events interacted significantly with unexpected death but was not predictive on its own. Parkes (1990: 309) summarizes studies of risk factors as follows:

> In short, statistical studies confirm what common sense leads one to suspect – that secure people whose experience of life has led to a reasonable trust in themselves, and others, will cope well with anticipated bereavements, provided they are well supported by a family who respects their need to grieve. However, multiple or unexpected and untimely losses of people on whom one depends or who depended on the survivor can overwhelm the most secure person and lack of security and support can undermine a person's capacity to cope with all types of bereavement.

If one factor does emerge as pre-eminent it is the perceived lack of social support (Stroebe and Stroebe 1987; Sanders 1988).

The use of risk factors to assess need

As described in Chapter 5, there are a number of limitations in the research literature and, while the case for targeting bereavement services on those most in need has been strongly argued (Parkes 1980, 1993a) their application in clinical practice remains problematic. The case for risk assessment includes ensuring that limited financial resources are used effectively and that the appropriate level of support is offered. It could be dangerous, for example, to offer volunteer support to a bereaved person with recent psychological problems. On the other hand, to offer counselling to someone who lacks social support may cause them to question their own ability to cope. Using risk factors to assess need enables services to be allocated using objective criteria rather than clinical judgements or 'gut feelings' alone. While the latter may be finely tuned, there is a danger that support may be offered to people for personal reasons. They may, for example, remind us of someone we know.

Parkes developed a risk index to enable nursing staff to identify those 'at risk' (see Parkes 1981; Parkes and Weiss 1983). This index provides a numerical score which is used to divide those at 'high risk' from those at 'low risk'. In his study of the St Christopher's Hospice bereavement service, approximately one third of key carers were assessed as 'at risk' using this index, all of whom were referred to the care of volunteers (Parkes 1981). This index is widely used in palliative care, both in its original and in adapted forms (Payne and Relf 1994). However, two studies examining the use of the original index have reported only limited support for its reliability as a predictive tool. Beckwith *et al.* (1990) found that it was predictive of outcome at three months after bereavement but not at one, six or twelve months. Levy *et al.* (1992) examined the internal validity of the index as well as its reliability. They found that the internal consistency was low (Cronbach's alpha = 0.50) and concluded that it could not be relied upon as a predictor of outcome and that the reasons for this lay in the instrument itself. It would seem, therefore, that the index contains flaws which may reflect the fact that the original index was derived from a study of young widows and widowers (Parkes and Weiss 1983) and was designed for settings where informal carers would become well-known to nursing staff over a period of time. Admissions are becoming shorter, even in hospices, and it may be difficult for nursing staff to feel that they have adequate understanding of the relevant issues. Moreover, informal carers may be unwilling to talk about their own needs at a time when their concerns may lie with the patient.

Payne and Relf (1994) surveyed 397 hospices, listed in the Hospice Directory (St Christopher's Hospice Information Science 1992) as having bereavement services, in order to examine the assessment of need for bereavement follow-up. In practice less than a third of respondents were using standardized assessment tools, usually based on Parkes' index. The remainder either relied on informal procedures (37 per cent), such as team discussions and clinical experience, or made no assessment, preferring to offer support to all (25 per cent). Some nurses viewed asking questions pertaining to risk assessment as intrusive. However, there were fewer problems associated with using a risk index than there were with relying on subjective assessments of need.

In summary, the use of risk indexes needs further refinement. In our experience of using an adapted version of Parkes' risk index in a palliative care setting over ten years, they have many advantages. However, staff need training before they can use risk indexes and need regular opportunities to discuss their assessments as well as completing a form. Existing risk indexes cannot be used alone but need to be part of an integrated system of training, discussion about assessments and checks. Whether or not an index is used, however, a knowledge of risk factors is likely to help proactive services target their resources more efficiently and help reactive services assess referrals and ensure that bereaved people receive appropriate interventions.

The assessment of need for intervention

A key issue for bereavement care, in particular for services designed to offer support, is the identification of need. Bereavement may cause great distress and, as discussed in Chapter 2, a substantial minority of bereaved people experience long-term disruption to their physical and psychological well-being and social functioning. Although the majority of bereaved people may be able to manage with the help of family and friends (Parkes 1993a), especially when good preparation and support has been received prior to the death, there remains a substantial minority of people who may be 'at risk'.

One branch of bereavement research has focused on identifying the factors associated with long-term health and social problems. These studies suggest that coping with bereavement is a dynamic process influenced by existing resources both intra- and interpersonal as well as the circumstances of the death. It has been demonstrated that it is possible to identify people who may be 'at risk' and a number of controlled studies have shown that offering preventive support to such people significantly reduces the likelihood that health and well-being will be compromised in the long term (see Parkes 1980). For example, Raphael (1977) found that professional counselling significantly reduced the number of physician visits, improved general health and reduced the consumption of alcohol, tobacco and psychotropic drugs. This was particularly true for widows who perceived their families as unsupportive. Raphael concluded that, although counselling had been offered by a psychiatrist, this level of training was not necessary to produce similar results. Indeed, Parkes (1981) found similar results when evaluating the St Christopher's Hospice bereavement service. He reported that 'at risk' bereaved people, supported by trained volunteers, had significantly fewer autonomic symptoms, consumed less alcohol and tobacco and were prescribed fewer drugs. Relf (1997) compared the health outcomes of supported and unsupported 'at risk' bereaved people and found that volunteer support significantly reduced the level of general practitioner consultations in the first year of bereavement and lowered levels of anxiety.

Bereavement services

Those whose grief is following an unexpectedly difficult course may seek or be recommended for therapeutic counselling in order to give them empathetic support while they grieve, or use a more structured approach, to help them grieve, with the idea that this will prevent difficulties later, or try to resolve grief which is causing severe and long-term problems. Concepts of complicated grief have already been discussed in Chapter 5. The approach used by most professional bereavement workers is usually predicated on the idea of helping people to work through various phases or tasks of grief which have been missed out or not completed, or to teach stress management and coping skills, or to help the bereaved to change maladaptive behaviour or cognitions. The approaches are found in a variety of settings in the community or in hospitals, and may be offered by a range of professionals. They may be described as bereavement therapy or bereavement counselling. Sometimes, the line between counselling and therapy is a fine one. Goodall *et al.* (1994: 135) offer the following distinctions:

◆ Counselling uses the basic skills of active listening.
◆ In contrast, therapy may make use of a wide range of additional skills and techniques.
◆ Counselling tends to be on an individual basis, while therapy may take place one-to-one or in groups.
◆ Bereavement therapy tends to be most appropriate for clients who have become stuck in their grief in some way.

It is beyond the scope of this book to describe in detail all possible approaches to bereavement counselling and therapy; Kavanagh (1990) describes cognitive behavioural approaches, and Raphael *et al.* (1993: 427–53) review a number of different techniques. Rather, a brief account will be given of some core techniques and research findings, ending by illustrating a widely-used therapeutic approach by describing its training programme, which is for counsellors wishing to gain specialist expertise in bereavement work, and is aimed at professionals seeking to develop skills in more structured interventions. The implicit and explicit assumptions behind the techniques will then be explored, and assessment of outcome will be considered. Issues specific to working with families were considered separately in Chapter 3.

The differing theoretical perspectives suggest that a variety of types of support may be needed by bereaved people. While the majority of bereaved people need understanding and general support, not all will need therapeutic counselling. The development of bereavement services reflects these varying levels of need, different views about the needs of bereaved people and how to provide bereavement care.

A number of different models of service provision have been developed and in recent years there has been a rapid expansion both within the community and within health care. Hospices have taken a leading role within health care (Faulkner 1993) and the majority have bereavement services to meet the demand for continuing support after patients' deaths (Wilkes 1993; Payne and Relf 1994). Some hospitals provide bereavement services and, as well as Cruse Bereavement Care which has branches throughout the UK, there are a growing number of independent community-based services. The latter are usually affiliated to the National Association of Bereavement Services. Services for bereaved children and their families are also being developed. A service that has attracted much attention is Winston's Wish which provides weekend camps for children and their parents, after-school groups and individual counselling (Stokes *et al.* 1997).

Provision and type of bereavement services

Bereavement services may be provided by:

◆ professionals such as GPs, counsellors, social workers, community psychiatric nurses, psychiatrists and psychologists;
◆ volunteers, usually with the support of professionals;
◆ mutual help groups run by bereaved people with or without the support of professionals.

These services may be:

◆ reactive – available only to those who ask for help or who are identified as having loss-related problems; or
◆ preventive – offered proactively to those who are likely to experience long-term difficulties.

Reactive services include the work of mental health professionals, trained counsellors and volunteer services that rely on self-referrals. The main example of the latter is Cruse Bereavement Care. Proactive services are found in settings where continuity of care may be provided, including hospitals, primary health care and palliative (hospice) care. They may also be offered by the clergy and bereavement services attached to churches. Parkes *et al.* (1996) describe the issues involved in providing preventive and proactive care in health care settings.

Professional services

Professionals with training in psychiatry, psychology, social work or counselling provide therapeutic bereavement counselling (Barbato and Irwin 1992; Lendrum and Syme 1992; Middleton *et al.* 1993) because 'complex risk situations are likely to require trained professional intervention' (Raphael and Nunn 1988: 199). Only a minority of bereaved people are likely to need this level of service. An obvious problem is knowing when grief has become so problematic that professional help is needed. As described in Chapter 5, grief may become problematic if it continues to disturb health and social functioning. Parkes (1985) has described lasting feelings of dejection, loss of purpose and meaning in life, social withdrawal, difficulty in concentration, impairment of memory and disturbances of appetite, weight and sleep as characteristic of this chronic phase. It is not simply a question of how much time has passed since the bereavement, but of how much disturbance of functioning is present, and whether it is resolving or staying unchanged or deepening. Bereaved people may be referred on to a psychiatrist if it is thought that the disturbance is of a kind requiring medication, or to a psychologist or psychotherapist if it is considered to be amenable to a behavioural approach or a 'talking cure'.

The advantages of professional involvement when grief becomes complicated are: that the suffering is legitimized and acknowledged as serious and beyond the scope of the grieving person to manage without skilled help; that a professional is neither surprised nor shocked by behaviour which may be viewed by others or the bereaved person as 'weak'; and that the person will be introduced to explanatory models for their suffering and to well-tried ways of dealing with it. The disadvantages are the implicit notion of 'illness' in being referred to a specialist, with its connotations of cure by an 'expert'. There are also concerns about the stigma of mental illness, an implicit perception that if a person needs psychological help they lack moral fibre, and a perception that failure to 'cope' is a weakness. These should be quickly dispelled in the first consultation, but can cause initial difficulty.

Cameron and Parkes' (1983) comparative study showed significant differences between the relatives of people who had died on a conventional ward and those who had died in a palliative care unit (PCU) which provided hospice-type care on the ward and at home, and which made one or two visits and telephone calls after the bereavement. Relatives of those who had died without that extra care were more irritable and angry and more hostile to others, slept worse and consumed more tranquillizers than the PCU group. However, it is difficult to interpret this study as it is unclear whether it was the bereavement care that made the difference or the fact that palliative care had been offered. Therefore it is safer not to draw firm conclusions.

Stronger evidence of the efficacy of psychiatric interventions following bereavement is provided by Raphael's work (1977). There is some evidence from these early studies that a relatively small amount of support over a short period often has a very positive effect on the subsequent course of bereavement, even in people identified in advance as being at high risk. These findings have shaped the current situation in which, in some countries at least, bereavement counselling in palliative care is commonplace, and professional services for unusually difficult or complicated bereavement are available. Issues around the provision of bereavement counselling by volunteers will be explored later in this chapter, and in the next section we address the characteristics and contribution of services and training offered by professionals.

The major approaches used in grief therapy (as distinct from supportive counselling) are, essentially, psychodynamic and cognitive-behavioural (which includes stress management). A typical psychodynamic approach is derived from the work of writers such as Freud and Klein and is based on the resolution of the ambivalence inherent in bereavement. Freud's belief was that disengagement (or decathexis) from the dead person is required so that the energy bound up in that relationship can be redirected to new relationships. Prolonged grief signals that disengagement has not taken place, and therapy is aimed at promoting a resolution of grief by means such as interpreting the client's feelings and exploring their defences with them, so that a more realistic appraisal of the loss may be made. Techniques such as abreaction and catharsis, which involve encouraging the expression of difficult emotions surrounding the loss, in the safe environment of therapy, may also be used. A summary of the major points of psychodynamic therapies for grief is given by Littlewood (1992: 63–5). A frequent criticism of this type of approach has been the lack of assessment of outcomes, but some research has been carried out. Marmar *et al.* (1988), for example, compared brief psychotherapy with a self-help group in a group of widows. The psychotherapy group showed an overall better outcome, which was maintained and possibly improved compared with the self-help group at follow-up, but there were different attrition rates, and unmatched samples, so it is difficult to draw any firm conclusions about relative efficacy.

Behavioural and cognitive-behavioural approaches

A variety of approaches based, at least conceptually, on behavioural techniques such as systematic desensitization or graded exposure, and the prevention or reversal of avoidance learning, have been developed. They typically also include elements of cognitive restructuring, stress management and coping skills. However, Kavanagh (1990) distinguishes between approaches based on graded exposure and habituation and more obviously cognitive interventions, and argues that the maintenance of depression is better explained from a cognitive perspective. Kavanagh characterizes chronic grief as 'an emotional feedback loop' (1990: 374) and points out that although there are many instances of exposure to multiple stimuli in bereavement they do not result in habituation. Kavanagh suggests that four kinds of skills, which will be present to some degree in many people's existing repertoire, are important in controlling transient sadness:

1 skills in 'grappling with the situation' and problem solving;
2 distraction and positive mood-induction skills;
3 skills in dealing with cognitive sources of negative mood;
4 skills in mobilizing assistance from other people.

Kavanagh proposes a model of intervention based on exploring the costs and benefits of change with the bereaved person, recognizing their existing skills, encouraging graded exposure to bereavement cues, graduated reinvolvement in roles and activities, and cognitive therapy (identifying and challenging negative thoughts) for excessively negative cognitions. In addition, strategies such as maximizing social support and limiting the use of drugs and alcohol are addressed. Kavanagh acknowledges that similar multifaceted interventions have been used by others, but believes that his places less emphasis on insight and interpretation and more on the training of coping skills than some psychodynamic models, and more emphasis on cognitive factors than some behavioural approaches.

Stroebe and Schut (1996) have developed a model of bereavement support based on theoretical concepts of coping derived from Lazarus and Folkman (1984) (described in Chapter 2). The model suggests that people vary in the extent to which their coping is problem-focused or emotion-focused. Using group work methods, Stroebe and Schut have implemented an intervention which takes account of individual coping styles, and encourages people to develop a range of coping strategies, especially those which they less typically use. For example, if a bereaved person responds to grief with problem-focused distraction strategies such as overworking and remaining continually engaged in tasks, they can be encouraged to face the emotional aspects of their loss, and vice versa. Such emotional responses have been typically gender stereotyped, with the assumption that men cope by being problem-focused and women cope by being emotion-focused. These stereotypes have been challenged by Riches and Dawson (1997) in parental grief responses following childhood deaths.

Another framework used by many bereavement services for understanding how individuals express grief is called dimensions of loss. The dimensions of loss were described in Chapter 5. The counsellor considers which dimensions are being referred to by the bereaved person and where difficulties are being experienced. For example, if bereaved people are very sad and tearful but feel that they should be coping better and are ashamed by their tears, the emotional dimension may be problematic. Their lack of ease may be causing tension and stress and may be affecting their health (physical dimension) and their social relations (social dimension). Others may feel that the mourner does not want to talk about their loss and avoid the subject for fear of upsetting them. Their self-esteem is also likely to be low because they are not coping in the preferred way (identity dimension). On the other hand if bereaved people are at ease with the expression of emotions, this may be a resource to them, even though they may feel distressed. Their ease may encourage others to talk to them and share their grief, they may be experiencing less agitation, anxiety and tension and their identity may be stronger – they are honouring the memory of the deceased by expressing their loss. The dimensions may be used to guide discussion in order to ascertain how grief is affecting the individual and may help the counsellor to note change over time. Parkes *et al.* (1996: 149–53) provide a case study illustrating the use of the dimensions of loss.

In more recent years, patterns of intervention like that described by Kavanagh (1990) have become more widely used in bereavement services, and training packages have been developed aimed at giving therapists and counsellors a range of appropriate skills. For example, Goodall *et al.* (1994) offer *The Bereavement and Loss Training Manual* which contains schemes for working with 'uncomplicated' and 'complicated' grief, for a range of people from teaching staff with pastoral care responsibilities to qualified professionals with experience of bereavement work. Trainees are first introduced to the major models of grief including psychodynamic, cognitive, attachment theory, stress, illness/disease and sociobiological models. Phase and task models are used to explain grief as a process, and trainees are invited to think in terms of which task they have failed to complete when formulating their plan of intervention. The training exercises include introducing and trying out techniques for use with clients, such as guided mourning (habituation), opportunities to explore and express difficult emotions like anger, guilt and ambivalence (catharsis) and the use of symbolic actions to deal with unfinished business. The approach is thus best described as eclectic. It may be said to draw on concepts derived from psychodynamic models of decathexis, and/or behavioural models derived from systematic desensitization. It also encourages and facilitates coping skills, and promotes self-efficacy.

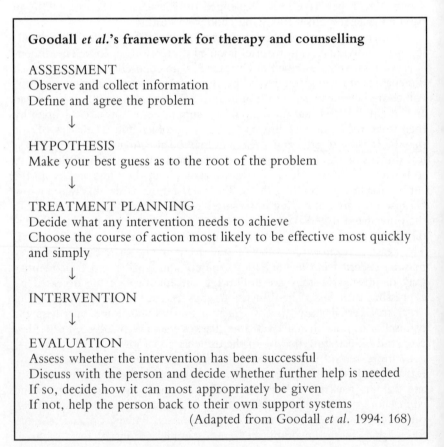

Goodall *et al.*'s framework for therapy and counselling

ASSESSMENT
Observe and collect information
Define and agree the problem
↓

HYPOTHESIS
Make your best guess as to the root of the problem
↓

TREATMENT PLANNING
Decide what any intervention needs to achieve
Choose the course of action most likely to be effective most quickly and simply
↓

INTERVENTION
↓

EVALUATION
Assess whether the intervention has been successful
Discuss with the person and decide whether further help is needed
If so, decide how it can most appropriately be given
If not, help the person back to their own support systems
(Adapted from Goodall *et al.* 1994: 168)

The manual includes sections on the needs of different client groups – for example, children and people with learning disabilities – and on grief associated with different kinds of loss, such as adoption, terminal illness or caring for someone with Alzheimer's disease. Issues of supervision and personal care are also addressed.

Goodall *et al.*'s (1994) example of a broad model for training bereavement therapists and counsellors contains some underlying assumptions:

♦ There is a need for personal development on the part of trainees in that workshop participants are asked to explore and share their own losses, feelings and coping strategies.
♦ The methods require the adoption of and competence in certain core skills, derived from client-centred counselling.
♦ The model of intervention is essentially based on two well-known and widely propagated models of grief (stage and task) derived from clinical observations rather than empirical studies, but its focus is present pain and difficulty and how best to alleviate them.
♦ It delineates normal and abnormal grief in terms of suffering and its impact on the life of the bereaved person and those closely involved.
♦ It uses the concept of grief to cover reactions to a variety of losses, not just death.
♦ It deals explicitly with the stress and potential for burnout in working with people with high levels of distress by addressing personal awareness and care issues during training and afterwards in working practices. (Burnout will be discussed further at the end of this section.)
♦ It is concerned with the maintenance of standards, through supervision (which also addresses personal care).
♦ It addresses the issue of limits of competence and when to refer-on.

Volunteer services

While professionals regularly see bereaved people, volunteers play a major role in both proactive and reactive services. In general, their role is more limited in scope than that of professionals. They are not usually expected to deal with pathological grief reactions and their training is not viewed as equipping them to deal with other problems not connected with the crisis of bereavement (Stewart 1994).

There are many advantages to involving volunteers. They:

♦ are members of the community and demonstrate that grief is a normal response to bereavement;
♦ carry none of the stigma attached to mental health services and may be perceived as less distant or less threatening than professionals;
♦ understand and represent the local community in a way that professionals cannot;

+ help spread knowledge about loss and bereavement among others in the community;
+ may be cost-effective (Parkes 1981; Relf 1997).

However, bereavement services that rely on volunteers need to be organized in a professional manner and have a sophisticated approach. Grief may be complex, and providing support may at times be problematic. Volunteers need to understand grief, be able to assess the level of need, have good listening and counselling skills and know their limits. A willingness to work with bereaved people is not sufficient. It is recommended that volunteers, working with both reactive and proactive services, should be carefully selected and work within a structure that provides safety both for themselves and their bereaved clients (Stewart 1994). This includes satisfactorily completing a training programme, attending supervision sessions, and further training. In other words, services that rely on volunteers should not be amateur services (Monroe 1993). It is not our intention to discuss the recruitment, selection, training and supervision of volunteers in detail here. However, it is important to note that attaining the recommended standards means that volunteer services need to be adequately coordinated: referrals need to be assessed to ensure that they fall within the capabilities of the volunteers' field; volunteers need to be recruited and provided with training and supervision; funding bodies are likely to require that the work is monitored and audited. Volunteer services, therefore, need resources to secure the back-up of trainers and supervisors with an appropriate professional background. Obtaining sufficient resources to attain the recommended standards is a key issue for volunteer services. For example, surveys have shown that hospice services may lack such resources (Wilkes 1993; Payne and Relf 1994). While some have been able to attract funds to employ a coordinator and administrator and pay for additional trainers and supervisors, others continue to rely on professionals being willing to volunteer their time. This means that volunteer services vary; some may provide befrienders with little training or supervision while others may be able to offer sophisticated levels of support and some require volunteers to have counselling qualifications and may be able to offer therapeutic counselling.

Mutual help

According to this model, bereaved people who are no longer experiencing acute grief themselves are in the best position to provide support to other bereaved people. By sharing experiences, talking about their loss and what helps, coping strategies are nurtured and inner strengths developed. Support is also provided through companionship, and mutual help groups often organize regular social events, such as going out for meals and to pubs. It may be easier to negotiate such events in the company of other bereaved people who understand the difficulties of managing a social life without the deceased. Examples of mutual help groups include the widow-to-widow programmes in the USA (Silverman 1970), and the worldwide Compassionate Friends (for bereaved parents). Usually the impetus for mutual help groups comes from bereaved people.

Burnout

Those who choose to work with bereaved people, either in a voluntary or a professional capacity, are of necessity in contact with the grief and distress of others day after day. They face the bitterness of death; the loneliness; the fear; the anger in their clients and patients; and they must face it without reacting other than with professionalism and compassion. Day after day, they are reminded of the inevitability of death, for their own loved ones and themselves, and of the deep and sometimes destructive sorrow that may come in its wake. Few would deny that these are hard tasks. On the one hand, those who work with the bereaved have chosen to do so, and studies have indicated that among the positive aspects of such work reported by volunteers and professionals are 'mastery' over their own previous losses (Garfield and Jenkins 1981–2); benefits in terms of coping with death (Robbins 1992); a sense of fulfilment; and a sense of privilege (Brotherton 1997). On the other hand, they are constantly 'giving' to clients, and are in the classic situation described first by Freudenberger (1974) and later developed by Maslach (1982) as producing risk of burnout. Maslach defined burnout as a syndrome of emotional exhaustion, depersonalization and reduced personal accomplishment that can occur among individuals who do 'people' work. She talked of the chronic emotional strain of dealing extensively with troubled human beings. Barni et al. (1996) differentiate burnout from other forms of occupational stress, suggesting that the nature of the interpersonal relationships at the core of the helping professions produces a particular set of stressors. The precise conditions under which burnout develops in some individuals have been investigated by a number of researchers, and include both environmental and individual factors. Results do not appear to be consistent across studies; Masterson-Allen et al. (1985) found that burnout was associated with length of employment in hospice staff, whereas Vachon (1978) found high levels of stress in nurses newly employed in a PCU. Thus one set of risk factors may be associated with accumulated stress and another with lack of experience and insufficiently developed coping skills. Ramirez et al. (1996) also found that perceived insufficient training in communication and management skills was related to burnout in palliative care physicians. Other studies have found personality characteristics to be a factor (e.g. Kash and Holland 1989) and coping style (e.g. Peteet et al. 1989). Protective factors include social support at work (Eastburg et al. 1994) and at home (Yasko 1983), coping skills (Whippen and Canellos 1991), and training (Ramirez et al. 1996). Vafeiadou

(1997) has drawn attention to the role of job satisfaction and a sense of personal accomplishment as antidotes to stress in oncology staff, together with clearly defined tasks and goals and a sense of control at work. Glass and McKnight (1996), in reviewing the evidence for perceived control as a key concept in burnout research, suggest that the association between the two is 'modest'. They posit frustrated achievement-striving as an issue worthy of further study in burnout, and also point to the need for prospective studies in the area.

Although these and other results appear to suggest multiple factors in the onset of burnout, the themes of personal competence, control and social support seem to be central in health care more generally, and in those working at the interface with death, the development of a personal philosophy (e.g. Chiriboga et al. 1983) is also important. Indeed, the nature of the work itself is seen by many as enabling the finding of meaning in life and in coming to terms with death. Models of working which include attention to training and supervision, not just at the outset but throughout one's working life, and definition and organization of tasks so as to promote a sense of competence and control seem to be important in enabling those who work with the dying and bereaved to derive a sense of fulfilment and satisfaction.

What is bereavement counselling?

The term 'bereavement counselling' is often used indiscriminately to refer to the range of services referred to above, spanning the continuum from compassionate communication to in-depth psychiatric management (Raphael et al. 1993). It is also used to refer to the many different strategies of support that bereavement services may employ. For example, hospice bereavement services include telephone and face-to-face support, therapeutic counselling, social activities, therapeutic groups and memorial services even though the central focus is one-to-one support (Wilkes 1993). In the wider field 'counselling' is used to refer to both the highly skilled therapeutic approaches that require extensive training and psychological insight, and to a supportive way of helping people (Davis and Fallowfield 1991; Feltham 1995). In the field of bereavement care, professionals generally provide therapeutic counselling while volunteers provide supportive counselling in the sense of 'giving time and attention, listening to and sharing a problem, perhaps . . . helping to unravel it and maybe make a decision about it' (Tyndall 1993: 10).

The generic use of 'bereavement counselling' to cover both therapeutic and supportive interventions causes confusion and there is an ongoing debate about whether volunteers should be referred to as 'bereavement counsellors'. On the one hand it is proposed that only those who have completed a certificate or diploma in counselling may call themselves counsellors. Others argue that 'counsellor' is an appropriate title for those who have had some specialized training and work under supervision. Many proactive services, such as hospice bereavement services, see their role as offering support rather than counselling. Their role is preventive and those they contact have not usually requested intervention. To offer 'counselling' proactively may lead some bereaved people to feel that grief is an illness rather than a natural reaction to bereavement. Indeed, hospice bereavement services often do not refer to their volunteers as counsellors (Wilkes 1993). It may be more appropriate that reactive services, such as Cruse Bereavement Care, describe their volunteers as counsellors as they are responding to requests for help. However, it must not be assumed that their volunteers have more training than those working for hospices.

The confusion about bereavement counselling is exacerbated by the lack of differentiation in the literature between the work of volunteers and that of professionals. Parkes and Worden describe the purpose of grief counselling as facilitating 'normal' grief. Worden (1982, 1991) sees this as primarily the role of mental health professionals and merely acknowledges the key role of volunteers while Parkes (1980) believes that volunteers are more than capable of providing bereavement counselling. He believes that, with experience, they may become highly skilled and tackle 'pathological' reactions. This view of volunteers as quasi-professional counsellors is widely held in the counselling field (Tyndall 1993). Stanners (1987), for example, refers to volunteer counsellors working with Cruse Bereavement Care as professionals because they are selected and trained for the work, possess specific theoretical knowledge and adhere to a code of ethics. It is not possible, therefore, to draw a clear line between the work of volunteers and that of professionals.

It is not surprising that views about who needs bereavement counselling and what counselling encompasses also vary. According to Worden (1991), the goals of grief counselling are to:

- increase the reality of the loss;
- help the counsellee deal with both expressed and latent affect;
- help the counsellee overcome various impediments to readjustment after the loss;
- encourage the counsellee to say an appropriate goodbye and to feel comfortable reinvesting back into life.

These goals reflect Worden's task-based model of grief and the grief work hypothesis. According to this perspective, mourners need to engage with their grief and work through their pain in order to adapt successfully. Proactive bereavement services, on the other hand, have adopted the view that some bereaved people may need support to help them through a stressful period of transition. As such they may see their role as wider than that described by Worden. For example, according to Lattanzi (1982: 56) hospice bereavement services have the following goals:

- to provide information about grief;
- to provide grieving family members with an opportunity to review and reflect on the experience of caring for their loved one and their loss;
- to assess and monitor individual coping ability;
- to encourage the use of existing support systems or to seek and create additional sources of support.

There is some evidence from empirical studies that simple supportive interventions are often effective in assisting people through the early stages of grief, and they can also reduce the risk of poor outcome in some high-risk groups. It is likely, although not proven, that complicated or long-term grief can be assisted by interventions such as those described above. The difficulty comes in attempting to determine which parts of the packages are effective in what circumstances. On a common-sense level, if anger is identified as a problem we might expect that an intervention specifically directed at resolving it would be most likely to be effective, but at this moment we cannot know for sure if this is so, or if, say, non-judgemental support would work just as well, because the studies have not been carried out. It is difficult to evaluate complex programmes of intervention when the use of comparison groups is impractical or unethical. We cannot invent a dummy therapy and it may be difficult to put a distressed and potentially at-risk person into a randomly-allocated no-treatment or 'other' condition in order to satisfy the requirements of a randomized controlled trial, although some randomized controlled trials have been undertaken. However, there are other models of systematic scientific enquiry which can and should be used to explore the efficacy of bereavement counselling and therapy, as the next step in its development. Prospective longitudinal studies with valid and reliable outcome measures would illuminate the core issues, and the use of reflective reports on the process and what was perceived as useful is as good a way as any to obtain data on what is, after all, the subjective experience of grief. Relf (1998) has begun this work and further details will be provided later in this chapter.

How do people respond to intervention?

While the literature on bereavement is extensive, there have been few studies of bereavement services. As mentioned in the previous section, a number of controlled studies have shown that proactive services, provided by both professionals and volunteers, may reduce health deterioration (Raphael 1977; Parkes 1981; Relf 1997). However, few studies have examined the process of providing support or counselling and little is known about the views of clients, how those providing support approach the work, or whether there are differences in need between different groups of bereaved people. For example, do gender or age have an impact on the take-up and use of services? There seems to be great variety in take-up rates of proactive services. Whereas the Sobell House bereavement service reports consistently high take-up rates of between 75 and 85 per cent per annum (*Annual Reports* of Sir Michael Sobell House, personal communication 1986–96) other hospices report much lower acceptance rates. For example, Gorman (1995) found that only 20 per cent of clients accepted support from the Ty Olwen hospice bereavement service.

Relf's (1997) study of the Sobell House bereavement service consisted of three parts. The first was a controlled study comparing the outcomes of supported and unsupported 'at risk' bereaved people. The second was a client opinion survey exploring 48 clients' responses to support. The third examined the process of providing a service from the volunteers' perspectives and consisted of interviews with volunteers throughout their involvement with 12 individual cases. The study provides further evidence that volunteer support does make a difference to the well-being of bereaved people. The results of the outcome evaluation were encouraging, showing that volunteer support had reduced the use of health care services (p=0.02), particularly GPs (p=0.03) and lowered anxiety. Fifty per cent of the control group saw their GP eight times or more during the first year of bereavement, whereas 90 per cent of the intervention group saw their GP less than four times. However, the second and third parts of the study revealed that previous conclusions that bereavement support is effective (Parkes 1980), were too global. Clients responded in three ways – while the majority welcomed the service some were more cautious and a minority were suspicious. The findings of the third part illustrated the diversity of clients' reactions and the impact of the work on the volunteers, and their need for support and supervision.

The second part of the study revealed that very few clients refused support but the use of the service varied from a couple of contacts to regular visits extending over as many as 18 months. The majority, over 75 per cent, were satisfied with support and saw their volunteers regularly, averaging ten visits. Four themes emerged from clients' descriptions of what was helpful:

1 being listened to;
2 feeling understood;
3 talking to someone who was not part of their social network;
4 information about grief.

Twenty-five per cent were less satisfied, tending to describe their support as social rather than emotional or indicating that they did not want to dwell on their grief. Four people found that being offered support was a painful reminder of all they were struggling to control and only accepted two or three visits. Establishing trust was not always easy, even among those clients who came to value support highly. This supports the conclusions of the majority of studies of social support and counselling. Efficacy seemed to be associated with the quality of the relationship and this reflects rapport and the demonstration of understanding through empathy.

Relf (1998) described a number of factors that may have influenced bereaved people's preparedness to enter into a relationship with their volunteer. According to Walter (1997b), keeping grief private is the accepted style of mourning in late modern societies. He suggests that the emphasis on independence and autonomy is at odds with the view that expressing grief is necessary for healthy adjustment. He argues that only those who are emotionally expressive fit with the expectations of bereavement services, whether reactive or proactive, professional or lay. Whereas more clients in Relf's (1998) study accepted support than Walter would seem to predict, Walter's observations offer an explanation for the fact that some clients were immediately open with their volunteers whereas others took time to develop trust and in some cases this proved impossible. In effect the volunteer's task is to become included in the client's private world. Volunteers were able to do so, but not with all their clients.

In Relf's (1998) study, some of the less satisfied clients viewed support as social. It must be remembered that volunteers have also been socialized in a culture that ascribes value to stoicism. They may get caught up in the client's initial uncertainty about accepting support and, therefore, find it hard to risk taking the conversation into potentially painful areas. The volunteer may simply follow the client's lead. The volunteer interviews revealed one instance where this was clearly the case. Relf concluded that the ability to respond to what may be implicitly, as well as explicitly, communicated marks the difference between support that provides social companionship and distraction from grief, and support that enables clients to feel understood and more able to cope. The capacity to do so may reflect the volunteer's level of skill. Inexperienced volunteers were more anxious about being accepted and saying the right things, whereas experienced volunteers were more focused on their clients. The study clearly illustrated the need for support and supervision. Indeed, the evaluation led to changes in both these aspects of the service.

Relf (1998) suggests that the quality of support and the effectiveness of bereavement care is influenced by the interplay between the client's coping style and beliefs about mourning, and the volunteer's skill and experience as well as their knowledge and understanding about grief. Hence, the ingredients of an effective service are not fixed, as previous outcome studies assume. Effective bereavement support depends upon the establishment of a relationship that demonstrates an understanding of the bereaved person, provides information about grief and provides sensitive companionship as the client struggles to adapt to their changed circumstances. Relf's volunteer interviews reveal that the focus was not necessarily on the facilitation of emotional discharge, although clients were often emotional. Neither was a correct way of mourning assumed, although the volunteers drew on models to explain features of grief that their clients were struggling to understand. Clearly, the 'grief work' model was insufficient both to explain the range of responses encountered by the volunteers and how they should respond. The DPM (Stroebe and Schut 1996), by introducing the concept of oscillation and describing the role of restoration-oriented behaviour, provided a more robust understanding of the diversity of reactions, in particular by normalizing a degree of avoidance and low distress. The dimensions of loss proved to be a more than adequate day-to-day framework for understanding how 'this grief' affects 'this individual'.

While indicating some features associated with the provision of support, Relf (1998) only began to explore the process, and further research is needed to confirm her findings and to examine the content of support more closely. There remains a paucity of research, particularly examining reactive bereavement services. The provision of bereavement care remains poorly understood.

Conclusion

When someone dies, the world of those closest to them changes, often in far-reaching ways. There is work to be done to adjust to the change and to deal with the loss. Although the focus of that work is with a few individuals, the larger social group is also affected; its integrity is threatened by the loss, and it will have a set of prescribed behaviours and rituals with a dual purpose: to acknowledge the life of the deceased group member and to restate the ongoing life of the group. For all that we know, raw grief, the 'reaction, emotional and behavioural' which is set in chain 'when a love-tie is severed' (Parkes 1986) has changed little over the years of human development, but societies and the way they conceptualize and deal with death have changed a great deal, more so in some parts of the world than in others. There are now very diverse ways of dealing with death and its aftermath across the world; some groups encourage the open expression of emotion, others discourage it. Some groups have elaborate rituals, others do not. In some societies mourning behaviour is tightly prescribed in both length and structure, and in others there is no such prescription. In the West, in countries characterized by certain types of technological advances, we have seen a significant change over the last 200 years or so. Dying, death and grief were once the province of the family, neighbours and the Church. Now, numerous professions have an input into all stages of the end of life. In 'developed' countries like the USA and the UK, most people die in hospital rather than at home, and bodies are dealt with first by health and then by funeral professionals. Grief is no longer private; it has become an area of study and research by academics, and a reason for intervention by clinicians and others if it is considered to be complicated or pathological. These facets of modern life are neither good nor bad in and of themselves;

they simply reflect the current state of thinking in contemporary societies. They are good to the extent that they meet the needs of the individuals and the group in such a way that the chaos and threat engendered by death is contained and adjustment is facilitated. They are bad to the extent that the interests of powerful groups – who may be politicians, priests, academics or clinicians – are served at the expense of the interests of the individuals most closely concerned: the bereaved. During this century, we have witnessed the results of one kind of professional focus on death – the development of theoretical models of grief which have the inherent notion of right and wrong ways to 'do' it. These models have been influential and helpful in identifying and intervening in patterns of grief which are associated with long-term ill-health and dysfunction, but perhaps less than helpful in attempting to tidy up the normal processes of grief and bring them into the clinical/professional realm. Why 'treat' and 'cure' a normal, if disturbing and painful, condition of life?

Most recently, the focus has moved away from the rather prescriptive models of grief into consideration of the very diverse ways in which people experience and deal with significant loss. We have learned from societies with patterns of grief very different from our own that 'healthy' and 'right' behaviour has many variations, and should properly be judged by its outcome. The questions we need to ask of other cultures include: does the prevailing way of dealing with bereavement offer support to the people most closely concerned?; does it enable them to deal with their pain and then continue with their altered lives, having incorporated the lost one and their experience in some kind of meaningful schema?; does it have a means of recognizing those at real risk of poor outcome (in terms of mental and/ or physical health)?; and does it have effective ways of intervening in those exceptional cases? We cannot import the beliefs and rituals of other cultures who seem to be 'doing it better', but we can learn from others that, for example, perceived support facilitates dealing with grief.

Summary

- ◆ Most models of grief suggest that people need to engage with it and process or work through it in order to reorder their lives after bereavement.
- ◆ Risk factors have been identified for those likely to find dealing with grief exceptionally difficult, among which perceived lack of social support is a central concept.
- ◆ When grief becomes a source of deep unhappiness or ill-health in the long term, therapeutic intervention from volunteers or professionals may be needed.
- ◆ Models of addressing complicated grief include guided mourning, psychodynamic, behavioural, cognitive-behavioural and eclectic.

♦ The extent to which outcome has been systematically evaluated varies a great deal, but there is evidence for the efficacy of some interventions.
♦ The risk of burnout in those who work with the bereaved, in voluntary or professional capacities, needs to be addressed.

Further reading

Parkes, C.M., Relf, M. and Couldrick, A. (1996) *Counselling in Terminal Care and Bereavement*. Leicester: British Psychological Society.
Stroebe, M.S. and Schut, H. (1996) *A model for coping with grief and its practical applications for the bereavement counsellor*. Paper presented at the third St George's 'Dying, Death and Bereavement' conference, St George's Hospital medical school, London, 6 March.
Worden, J.W. (1991) *Grief Counselling and Grief Therapy: A Handbook for the Mental Health Practitioner*, 2nd edn. New York: Springer Publishing.

References

Ainsworth, M.D.S., Blehar, M.C., Waters, E. and Wall, S. (1978) *Patterns of Attachment*. Hilldale, NJ: Lawrence Erlbaum Associates.

Annwn, D. (1997) Journey. *Progress in Palliative Care*, 4(1): 9.

Archer, J. (1990) Have animal models contributed to studies of loss and separation? *The Psychologist*, 3(7): 298–301.

Averill, J.R. (1968) Grief: its nature and significance. *Psychological Bulletin*, 70(6): 721–48.

Ball, J.F. (1977) Widows' grief: the impact of age and mode of death. *Omega: Journal of Death and Dying*, 7: 307–33.

Bandura, A.A. (1977) *Social Learning Theory*. Englewood Cliffs, NJ: Prentice-Hall.

Bankoff, E.A. (1986) Peer support for widows: personal and structural characteristics related to its provision, in S.E. Hobfoll (ed.) *Stress, Social Support and Women*. Washington DC: Hemisphere.

Barbato, A. and Irwin, H.J. (1992) Major therapeutic systems and the bereaved client. *Australian Psychologist*, 27: 22–7.

Barni, S., Mondini, R., Nazzani, R. and Archili, C. (1996) Oncostress: evaluation of burnout in Lombardy. *Tumori*, 82(1): 85–92.

Barnlund, D. (1976) The mystification of meaning: doctor-patient encounters. *Journal of Medical Education*, 51: 716–25.

Bartlett, D. (1998) *Stress*. Buckingham: Open University Press.

Bates, M. (1987) Ethnicity and pain: a biocultural model. *Social Science and Medicine*, 24: 47–50.

Beckwith, B.E., Beckwith, S.K., Gray, T.L. *et al.* (1990) Identification of spouses at high risk during bereavement: a preliminary assessment of Parkes and Weiss' risk index. *The Hospice Journal*, 6(3): 35–45.

Berardo, F.M. (1970) Survivorship and social isolation: the case of the aged widower. *Family Co-ordinator*, 19: 11–25.

Berk, L.E. (1991) *Child Development*, 2nd edn. Needhan Heights MA: Allyn & Bacon.

Bonanno, G.A., Keltner, D., Holen, A. and Horowitz, M.J. (1995) When avoiding unpleasant emotions might not be such a bad thing: verbal-autonomic response dissociation and midlife conjugal bereavement. *Journal of Personality and Social Psychology*, 69(5): 975–89.

Book, P.L. (1996) How does family narrative influence the individual's ability to communicate about death? *Omega: Journal of Death and Dying*, 33(4): 323–41.

Boss, P. and Greenberg, J. (1984) Family boundary ambiguity: a new variable in family stress theory. *Family Process*, 23: 535–46.

Bowlby, J. (1960) Grief and mourning in infancy and early childhood. *Psychoanalytic Study of the Child*, 15: 9–52.

Bowlby, J. (1969) *Attachment and Loss, Vol. 1: Attachment*. London: The Hogarth Press.

Bowlby, J. (1973) *Attachment and Loss, Vol. 2: Separation*. London: The Hogarth Press.

Bowlby, J. (1980) *Attachment and Loss, Vol. 3: Loss – Sadness and Depression*. London: The Hogarth Press.

Bowlby, J. and Parkes, C.M. (1970) Separation and loss within the family, in E.J. Anthony and C. Koupernik (eds) *The Child in His Family*. New York: Wiley.

Brotherton, J. (1997) Stress, coping and death anxieties: an exploratory study of volunteers befriending the dying and bereaved. Unpublished Master's thesis, University of Southampton.

Brown, G.A. and Harris, T.A. (1978) *Social Origins of Depression: A Study of Psychiatric Disorder in Women*. New York: Free Press.

Bunch, J. (1972) Recent bereavement in relation to suicide. *Journal of Psychosomatic Research*, 16: 361–6.

Cacioppo, J.T., Anderson, B.L., Turnquist, D.C. and Petty, R.E. (1986) Psychophysiological comparison processes: interpreting cancer symptoms, in B.L. Andersen (ed.) *Women with Cancer*. New York: Springer-Verlag.

Cameron, J. and Parkes, C.M. (1983) Terminal care: evaluation of effects on surviving family of care before and after bereavement. *Postgraduate Medical Journal*, 59: 73–8.

Cannon, W.B. (1932) *The Wisdom of the Body*. New York: Norton.

Carroll, D., Niven, C.A. and Sheffield, D. (1993) Gender, social circumstances and health, in C.A. Niven and D. Carroll (eds) *The Health Psychology of Women*. Switzerland: Harwood Academic Publisher.

Carver, C.C., Scheier, M.F. and Weintraub, J.K. (1989) Assessing coping strategies: a theoretically based approach. *Journal of Personality and Social Psychology*, 56: 267–83.

Caserta, M.S. and Lund, D.A. (1992) Bereavement stress and coping among older adults: expectations versus the actual experience. *Omega: Journal of Death and Dying*, 25(1): 33–45.

Chase, P.G. and Dibble, H.L. (1987) Middle Paleolithic symbolism: a review of current evidence and interpretations. *Journal of Anthropological Archaeology*, 6: 263–96.

Chilman, C.S., Nunnally, E.W. and Cox, F.M. (1988) *Chronic Illness and Disability*. Newbury Park, CA: Sage.

Chiriboga, D.A., Jenkins, G. and Bailey, J. (1983) Stress and coping among hospice nurses: test of an analytic model. *Nursing Research*, 32, 294–9.

Christ, G.H. (1998) Outcomes of childhood bereavement. *Psycho-Oncology*, 4 (supplement): 187.

Clayton, P.J. (1974) Mortality and morbidity in the first year of widowhood. *Archives of General Psychiatry*, 30: 747–50.

Clayton, P.J. (1982) Bereavement, in E.S. Paykel (ed.) *Handbook of Affective Disorders*, pp. 403–15. New York: Guildford Press.

Cleiren, M.P.H.D. (1991) *Bereavement and Adaptation: A Comparative Study of the Aftermath of a Death*. Washington: Hemisphere Publishing.

Conant, R.D. (1996) Memories of the death and life of a spouse: the role of images and sense of presence in grief, in D. Klass, P. Silverman and S.L. Nickman (eds) *Continuing Bonds*. Philadephia, PA: Taylor & Francis.

Cormack, M. (1996) Family functioning and spinal cord injury: an exploratory cluster analytic approach examining perceived family functioning and psychosocial adjustment to chronic disability. Unpublished MSc health psychology dissertation, University of Southampton.

Coyne, J.C. and DeLongis, A. (1986) Going beyond social support: the role of social relationships in adaption. *Journal of Consulting and Clinical Psychology*, 54(4): 454–60.

Davies, B., Spinetta, J. and Martinson, I. (1986) Manifestations of levels of functioning in bereaved families. *Journal of Family Issues*, 7: 297–313.

Davis, H. and Fallowfield, L. (1991) *Counselling and Communication in Health Care*. Chichester: John Wiley & Sons.

Deutsch, H. (1937) Absence of grief. *Psycho-Analytic Quarterly*, 6: 12–22.

DeVaul, R.A., Zisook, S. and Faschingbauer, T.R. (1979) Clinical aspects of grief and bereavement. *Primary Care*, 6: 391–402.

Eastburg, M.C., Williamson, M., Gorsuch, R. and Ridlay, C. (1994) Social support, personality and burnout in nurses. *Journal of Applied Social Psychology*, 24(14): 1233–50.

Eisenbruch, M. (1984a) Cross-cultural aspects of bereavement, I: a conceptual framework for comparative analysis. *Culture, Medicine and Psychiatry*, 8: 283–309.

Eisenbruch, M. (1984b) Cross-cultural aspects of bereavement, II: ethnic and cultural variations in the development of bereavement practices. *Culture, Medicine and Psychiatry*, 8: 315–47.

Eiser, C. (1990) *Chronic Childhood Disease*. Cambridge: Cambridge University Press.

Ellmann, L. (1994) Penance soup, in J. McLoughlin (ed.) *On the Death of a Parent*. London: Virago.

Engel, G.L. (1961) Is grief a disease? *Psychosomatic Medicine*, 23: 18–22.

Erikson, E.H. (1963) *Childhood and Society*, 2nd edn. New York: Norton.

Etchells, R. (1988) *A Selection from the Early English Poets*. Tring: Lion Publishing.

Faschingbauer, T.R., Zisook, S. and DeVaul, R.A. (1987) The Texas revised inventory of grief, in S. Zisook (ed.) *Biopsychosocial Aspects of Bereavement*. Washington, DC: American Psychiatric Press.

Faulkner, A. (1993) Developments in bereavement services, in D. Clark (ed.) *The Future for Palliative Care: Issues of Policy and Practice*. Buckingham: Open University Press.

Feifel, H. (1998) Grief and bereavement. *Bereavement Care*, 7(1): 2–4.

Feltham, C. (1995) *What is Counselling?* London: Sage.

Fenichel, O. (1945) *The Psychoanalytic Theory of Neurosis*. New York: Norton.

Field, D., Hockey, J. and Small, N. (eds) (1997) *Death, Gender and Ethnicity*. London: Routledge.

Firth, R. (1961) *Elements of Social Organisation*, 3rd edn. London: Tavistock.

Firth, S. (1993) Cultural issues in terminal care, in D. Clark (ed.) *The Future for Palliative Care: Issues of Policy and Practice*. Buckingham: Open University Press.

Fisher, L., Howard, E.T. and Ransom, D.C. (1990) Advancing a family perspective in health research: models and methods. *Family Process*, 29(2): 177–89.

Fitchett, G. (1980) It's time to bury the stage theory of death and dying. *Oncology Nurse Exchange*, 2: 3.

Ford, F.R. (1983) Rules: the invisible family. *Family Process*, 22(2): 135–45.

Foster, M. (1998) *Precious Lives*. London: Chatto & Windus.

Foucault, M. (1973) *The Birth of the Clinic: An Archaeology of Medical Perception*, trans. A. Sheridan. London: Tavistock.

Frank, A. (1991) *At the Will of the Body*. Boston: Houghton Mifflin.

Freud, S. (1917) *Mourning and Melancholia, Collected Papers*, Vol. 4. New York: Basic Books.

Freudenberger, H.J. (1974) Staff burnout. *Journal of Social Issues*, 30: 159–65.

Gale, A. and Barker, M. (1987) The repertory grid approach to analysing family members' perception of self and others: a pilot study. *Journal of Family Therapy*, 9: 355–66.

Gallagher-Thompson, D.E., Futterman, A., Farbarrow, N. and Peterson, J.A. (1993) The impact of spousal bereavement on older widows and widowers, in M.S. Stroebe, W. Stroebe and R.O. Hansson (eds) *Handbook of Bereavement*. Cambridge: Cambridge University Press.

Garfield, C.A. and Jenkins, G.J. (1981–2) Stress and coping of volunteers counseling the dying and bereaved. *Omega: Journal of Death and Dying*, 12(1): 1–13.

Gelcer, E. (1983) Mourning is a family affair. *Family Process*, 22: 501–16.

Giddens, A. (1991) *Modernity and Self-Identity*. Cambridge: Polity Press.

Glass, D.C. and McKnight, J.D. (1996) Perceived control, depressive symptomatology, and professional burnout: a review of the evidence. *Psychology and Health*, 11(1): 23–48.

Glick, I., Weiss, R. and Parkes, C.M. (1974) *The First Year of Bereavement*. New York: John Wiley & Sons.

Goldstein, R.D., Wampler, N.S. and Wise, P.H. (1997) War experiences and distress symptoms of Bosnian children. *Pediatrics*, 100(5): 873–8.

Golsworthy, R. and Colye, A. (1999) Spiritual beliefs and the search for meaning among older adults following partner loss. *Mortality*, 4(1): 21–40.

Goodall, A., Drage, T. and Bell, G. (1994) *The Bereavement and Loss Training Manual*. Bicester: Winslow Press Ltd.

Gorer, G. (1965) *Death, Grief and Mourning in Contemporary Britain*. London: Cresset Press.

Gorman, A. (1995) An evaluation of a bereavement support service. *Palliative Care Today*, 4: 38–9.

Gotay, C. (1996) Cultural variations in family adjustment to cancer, in L. Baider, C.L. Cooper and A. De-Nour (eds) *Cancer and the Family*. Chichester: John Wiley & Sons.

Grainger, R. (1998) *The Social Symbolism of Grief and Mourning*. London: Jessica Kinglsey.

Graves, R. (1955) *The Greek Myths: 1*. Harmondsworth: Penguin.

Harlow, H.F., Gluck, J.P. and Suomi, S.J. (1972) Generalization of behavioural data between nonhuman and human animals. *American Psychologist*, August: 709–16.

Harrington, R. and Harrison, L. (1999) Unproven assumptions about the impact of bereavement on children. *Journal of the Royal Society of Medicine*, 92: 230–3.

Helsing, K.J. and Szklo M. (1981). Mortality after bereavement. *American Journal of Epidemiology*, 114: 41–52.

Herbert, M. (1988) *Working With Children and Their Families*. London: Routledge/BPS Books.

Herbert, T.B. and Cohen, S. (1993) Stress and immunity in humans: a meta-analytic review. *Psychosomatic Medicine*, 55: 364–79.

Hewson, D. (1997) Coping with the loss of ability: 'good grief' or episodic stress responses? *Social Science and Medicine*, 44(8): 1129–39.

Hill, R. (1966) Contemporary developments in family theory. *Journal of Marriage and the Family*, 28, 10–25.

Hill, S. (1989) *Family*. London: Michael Joseph.

Hockey, J. (1997) Woman in grief: cultural representation and social practice, in D. Field, J. Hockey and N. Small (eds) *Death, Gender and Ethnicity*. London: Routledge.

Hofer, M.A. (1996) On the nature and consequences of early loss. *Psychosomatic Medicine*, 58: 570–81.

Hoffman, L. (1981) *Foundations of Family Therapy: A Conceptual Framework for Systems Change*. New York: Basic Books.

Holmes, T.H. and Rahe, R.H. (1967) The social readjustment scale. *Journal of Psychosomatic Research*, 11: 213–18.

Horowitz, J.C.M., Marmar, C., Weiss, D.S., DeWitt, K. and Rosenbaum, R. (1984) Brief psychotherapy of bereavement reactions. *Archives of General Psychiatry*, 41: 438–48.

Hubert, J. (1992) Dry bones or living ancestors? Conflicting perceptions of life, death and the universe. *International Journal of Cultural Property*, 1(1): 105–27.

Huntington, R. and Metcalf, P. (1979) *Celebrations of Death: The Anthropology of Mortuary Ritual*. Cambridge: Cambridge University Press.

Ironson, G., Wynings, C., Schneiderman, N. *et al.* (1997) Posttraumatic stress symptoms, intrusive thoughts, loss and immune function after Hurricane Andrew. *Psychosomatic Medicine*, 59(2): 128–41.

Jacobs, S., Hansen, F., Kasl, S. and Ostfeld, A. (1989) Depressions of bereavement. *Comprehensive Psychiatry*, 30(3): 218–24.

Johnson, J. (1988) Cancer: a family disruption. *Recent Results in Cancer Research*, 108: 306–10.

Johnson, M. (1996) *The Dead Citizen's Charter*. Stamford: National Funerals College.

Kalish, R.A. (1985) *Death, Grief and Caring Relationships*, 2nd edn. New York: Brooks Cole.

Kantor, D. and Lehr, W. (1975) *Inside the Family: Towards a Theory of Family Process*. San Francisco, CA: Jossey-Bass.

Kaprio, J., Koskenvuo, M. and Rita, H. (1987) Mortality after bereavement: a prospective study of 95,647 widowed persons. *American Journal of Public Health*, 77: 283–7.

Kash, K.M. and Holland, J.C. (1989) Special problems of physicians and house staff in oncology, in J.C. Holland and J.H. Rowland (eds) *Handbook of Psycho-oncology*. New York: Oxford University Press.

Kavanagh, D.J. (1990) Towards a cognitive-behavioural intervention for adult grief reactions. *British Journal of Psychiatry*, 157: 373–83.

Kazak, A. (1989) Families of chronically ill children: a systems and socio-ecological model of adaptation and challenge. *Journal of Consulting and Clinical Psychology*, 57(1): 25–30.

Kessler, R.C., Price, R.H. and Wortman, C. (1985) Social factors in psychopathology: stress, social support and coping processes. *Annual Review of Psychology*, 36: 531–72.

Kiecolt-Glaser, J.K. and Glaser, R. (1986) Psychological influences on immunity. *Psychosomatics*, 27: 621–4.

Kim, K. and Jacobs, S. (1993) Neuroendocrine changes following bereavement, in M.S. Stroebe, W. Stroebe and R.O. Hansson (eds) *Handbook of Bereavement*. Cambridge: Cambridge University Press.

King, M., Speck, P. and Thomas, A. (1994) Spiritual and religious beliefs in acute illness: is this a feasible area for study? *Social Science and Medicine*, 38(4): 631–6.

Kissane, D.W. and Bloch, S. (1984) Family grief. *British Journal of Psychiatry*, 164, 728–40.

Kissane, D.W., Bloch, S., Burns, W.I. *et al.* (1994) Perceptions of family functioning and cancer. *Psycho-oncology*, 3: 259–69.

Kissane, D.W., Bloch, ·S., Dowe, D.L. *et al.* (1996) The Melbourne family grief study 1: perceptions of family functioning in bereavement. *The American Journal of Psychiatry*, 153(5): 650–8.

Kissane, D.W., Bloch, S., McKenzie, M., McDowall, A.C. and Nitzan, R. (1998) Family grief therapy: a preliminary account of a new model to promote healthy family functioning during palliative care and bereavement. *Psycho-oncology*, 7: 14–25.

Klass, D. (1996) The deceased child in the psyche and social worlds of bereaved parents during the resolution of grief, in D. Klass, P. Silverman and S.L. Nickman (eds) *Continuing Bonds*. Philadelphia, PA: Taylor & Francis.

Klass, D. and Heath, A.O. (1996) Grief and abortion: Mizuko Kuyo, the Japanese ritual resolution. *Omega: Journal of Death and Dying*, 34(1): 1–14.

Klass, D., Silverman, P.R. and Nickman, S.L. (eds) (1996) *Continuing Bonds*. Philadelphia, PA: Taylor & Francis.

Kobasa, S.C. (1979) Stressful life events, personality and hardiness: an inquiry into hardiness. *Journal of Personality and Social Psychology*, 37: 1–11.

Kubler-Ross, E. (1969) *On Death and Dying*. New York: Macmillan.

Lantz, J. and Ahern, R. (1998) Re-collection in existential therapy with couples and families facing death. *Contemporary Family Therapy: An International Journal*, 20(1): 47–57.

Lattanzi, M.E. (1982) Hospice bereavement services: creating networks of support. *Family and Community Health*, 5: 54–63.

Laudenslager, M.L., Boccia M.L. and Reite, M.L. (1993) Biobehavioural consequences of loss in nonhuman primates: individual differences, in M.S. Stroebe, W. Stroebe and R.O. Hansson (eds) *Handbook of Bereavement*. Cambridge: Cambridge University Press.

Laungani, P. (1996) Death and bereavement in India and England: a comparative analysis. *Mortality*, 1(2): 191–212.

Laungani, P. (1997) Death in a Hindu family, in C.M. Parkes, P. Laungani and B. Young (eds) *Death and Bereavement Across Cultures*. London: Routledge.

Lazarus, R.S. (1996) *Psychological Stress and the Coping Process*. New York: McGraw-Hill.

Lazarus, R.S. and Folkman, S. (1984) *Stress, Appraisal and Coping*. New York: Springer-Verlag.

Lehman, D.R., Ellard, J.H. and Wortman, C. (1986) Social support for the bereaved: recipients' and providers' perspectives on what is helpful. *Journal of Consulting and Clinical Psychology*, 54: 438–46.

Lendrum, S. and Syme, G. (1992) *Gift of Tears*. London: Routledge.

Levine, E. (1997) Jewish views and customs on death, in C.M. Parkes, P. Laungani and B. Young (eds) *Death and Bereavement Across Cultures*. London: Routledge.

Levy, L.H., Derby, J.F. and Martwomski, K.S. (1992) The question of who participates in bereavement research and the bereavement risk index. *Omega: Journal of Death and Dying*, 25: 225–38.

Lewis, C.S. (1966) *A Grief Observed*. London: Faber & Faber.

Lindemann, E. (1944) Symptomatology and management of acute grief. *American Journal of Psychiatry*, 101: 141–8.

Lindstrom, T.C. (1997) Immunity and health after bereavement in relation to coping. *Scandinavian Journal of Psychology*, 38: 253–9.

Litten, J. (1997) The funeral trade in Hanoverian England 1714–1760, in P.C. Jupp and G. Howarth (eds) *The Changing Face of Death*. Basingstoke: Macmillan.

Littlewood, J. (1987) Bereavement status: a neglected area of research. Paper presented at the 'First International Conference on Multi-Disciplinary Aspects of Terminal Care', Glasgow, September.

Littlewood, J. (1992) *Aspects of Grief*. London: Routledge.

Lopata, H.Z. (1975) Grief work and identity reconstruction. *Journal of Geriatric Psychiatry and Neurology*, 8: 41–55.

Lopata, H.Z. (1979) *Women as Widows*. New York: Elsevier Science.

Lorenz, K. (1966) *On Aggression*. New York: Harcourt Brace Jovanovich.

Lovell, A. (1997) Death at the beginning of life, in D. Field, J. Hockey and N. Small (eds) *Death, Gender and Ethnicity*. London: Routledge.

Lund, D., Caserta, M.S. and Dimond, M.F. (1993) The course of spousal bereavement in later life, in M.S. Stroebe, W. Stroebe and R.O. Hansson (eds) *Handbook of Bereavement*. Cambridge: Cambridge University Press.

Lundin, T. (1984) Morbidity following sudden and unexpected bereavements. *British Journal of Psychiatry*, 144: 84–8.

McCrae, R. and Costa, P.T. (1993) Psychological resilience among widowed men and women: a ten-year follow-up of a national sample, in M.S. Stroebe, W. Stroebe and R.O. Hansson (eds) *Handbook of Bereavement*. Cambridge: Cambridge University Press.

MacElveen-Hoehn, P. (1993) Sexual responses to the stimulus of death, in J.D. Morgan (ed.) *Personal Care in an Impersonal World: A Multidimensional Look at Bereavement*. Amityville, NY: Baywood Publishing Company Inc.

Machin, L. (1996) Living with loss: a survey of the bereavement response of 97 people, in L. Machin and G. Pierce (eds) *Research: A Road to Good Practice*. Keele: University of Keele Centre for Counselling Studies.

McNicholas, J. and Collis, G.M. (1995) The end of a relationship: coping with pet loss, in I. Robinson (ed.) *The Waltham Book of Human-Animal Interaction*. Oxford: Pergamon Press.

Maddison, D.C. and Walker, W.L. (1967) Factors affecting the outcome of conjugal bereavement. *British Journal of Psychiatry*, 113: 1057–67.

Marmar, C.R., Horowitz, M.J., Weiss, D.S., Wilner, N.R. and Kaltreider, N.B. (1988) A controlled trial of brief psychotherapy and mutual-help group treatment of conjugal bereavement. *American Journal of Psychiatry*, 145(2): 203–12.

Marris, P. (1958) *Widows and their Families*. London: Routledge and Kegan Paul.

Marris, P. (1986) *Loss and Change*, 2nd edn. London: Routledge.

Marris, P. (1992) Grief, loss of meaning and society. *Bereavement Care*, 11(2): 18–23.

Marwit, S.J. and Klass, D. (1995) Grief and the role of the inner representation of the deceased. *Omega: Journal of Death and Dying*, 30: 283–98.

Maslach, C. (1982) *Burnout: the cost of caring*. Englewood Cliffs, NJ: Prentice-Hall.

Masterson-Allen, S., Mor, V., Laliberte, L. and Monteiro, L. (1985) Staff burnout in a hospice setting. *Hospice Journal*, 1: 1–15.

May, C. (1992) Individual case? Power and subjectivity in therapeutic relationships. *Sociology*, 26(4): 589–602.

Mendelson, M. (1982) Psychodynamics of depression, in E.S. Paykel (ed.) *Handbook of Affective Disorders*. London: Churchill and Livingston.

Middleton, W., Moylan, A., Burnett, P. and Martinek, N. (1991) An international perspective on bereavement related concepts. Paper presented at the 'Third International Conference on Grief and Bereavement in Contemporary Society', Sydney, Australia.

Middleton, W., Raphael, B., Martinek, N. and Misso, V. (1993) Pathological grief reactions, in M.S. Stroebe, W. Stroebe and R.O. Hansson (eds) *Handbook of Bereavement*. Cambridge: Cambridge University Press.

Monroe, B. (1993) Social work in palliative care, in D. Doyle, G.W.C. Hanks and N. Macdonald (eds) *Oxford Textbook of Palliative Medicine*. Oxford: Oxford University Press.

Nadeau, J.W. (1997) *Families Making Sense of Death Dysfunction*. Thousand Oaks, CA: Sage.

Normand, C.L., Silverman, P.R. and Nickman, S.L. (1996) Bereaved children's changing relationship with the deceased, in D. Klass, P.R. Silverman and S.L. Nickman (eds) *Continuing Bonds: New Understandings of Grief*. Washington, DC: Taylor & Francis.

Ogden, J. (1996) *Health Psychology: A Textbook*. Buckingham: Open University Press.

Olson, D.H., Sprenkle, D.H. and Russell, C.S. (1979) Circumplex model of marital and family systems, 1: cohesion and adaptability dimensions, family types and clinical applications. *Family Process*, 18(1): 3–28.

Osterweis, M., Solomon, F. and Green M. (eds) (1984) *Bereavement Reactions, Consequences and Care*. Washington, DC: National Academy Press.

Parkes, C.M. (1965a) Bereavement and mental illness, part 1: a clinical study of the grief of bereaved psychiatric patients; part 2: a classification of bereavement reactions. *British Journal of Medical Psychology*, 38: 388–97.

Parkes, C.M. (1965b) Bereavement and mental illness. *British Medical Journal*, 38: 1–26.

Parkes, C.M. (1970) The first year of bereavement: a longitudinal study of the reaction of London widows to the death of their husbands. *Psychiatry*, 33: 444–67.

Parkes, C.M. (1971) Psychosocial transitions: a field for study. *Social Science and Medicine*, 5(2): 101–14.

Parkes, C.M. (1972) *Bereavement: Studies of Grief in Adult Life*. Harmondsworth: Penguin.

Parkes, C.M. (1975) Unexpected and untimely bereavement: a statistical study of young Boston widows and widowers, in B.M. Schoenberg, I. Gerber, A. Weiner *et al.* (eds) *Bereavement: Its Psychological Aspects.* New York: Columbia University Press.

Parkes, C.M. (1980) Bereavement counselling: does it work? *British Medical Journal,* 281: 3–6.

Parkes, C.M. (1981) Evaluation of a bereavement service. *Journal of Preventive Psychiatry,* 1: 179–88.

Parkes, C.M. (1985) Bereavement. *British Journal of Psychiatry,* 146: 11–17.

Parkes, C.M. (1986) *Bereavement: Studies of Grief in Adult Life,* 2nd edn. London: Routledge.

Parkes, C.M. (1990) Risk factors in bereavement: implications for the prevention and treatment of pathologic grief. *Psychiatric Annals,* 20: 308–13.

Parkes, C.M. (1993a) Bereavement, in D. Doyle, G.W.C. Hanks and N. Macdonald (eds) *Oxford Textbook of Palliative Medicine.* Oxford: Oxford University Press.

Parkes, C.M. (1993b) Bereavement as a psychosocial transition: processes of adaption to change, in M.S. Stroebe, W. Stroebe and R.O. Hansson (eds) *Handbook of Bereavement.* Cambridge: Cambridge University Press.

Parkes, C.M. (1995) Attachment and bereavement. *Proceedings of the fourth international conference on grief and bereavement in contemporary society.* Stockholm: Swedish National Association for Mental Health.

Parkes, C.M. (1996) *Bereavement: Studies of Grief in Adult Life,* 3rd edn. London: Routledge.

Parkes, C.M. and Brown, R.J. (1972) Health after bereavement: a controlled study of young Boston widows and widowers. *Psychosomatic Medicine,* 34: 449–61.

Parkes, C.M. and Weiss, R.S. (1983) *Recovery from Bereavement.* New York: Basic Books.

Parkes, C.M., Relf, M. and Couldrick, A. (1996) *Counselling in Terminal Care and Bereavement.* Leicester: British Psychological Society.

Parkes, C.M., Laungani, P. and Young, B. (eds) (1997) *Death and Bereavement Across Cultures.* London: Routledge.

Payne, S. and Relf, M. (1994) A survey of bereavement needs assessment and support services. *Palliative Medicine,* 8: 291–7.

Pegg, P.F. and Metze, E. (eds) (1981) *Death and Dying: A Quality of Life.* Bath: Pitman.

Peteet, J.R., Murray-Ross, D., Medeiros, C. *et al.* (1989) Job stress and satisfaction among the staff members at a cancer center. *Cancer,* 64: 975–82.

Ramirez, A.J., Graham, J., Richards, M.A., Call, A. and Gregory, W.M. (1996) Mental health of hospital consultants: the effects of stress and satisfaction at work. *Lancet,* 347: 724–8.

Raphael, B. (1977) Preventive intervention with the recently bereaved. *Archives of General Psychiatry,* 34: 1450–4.

Raphael, B. (1980) A psychiatric model for counselling, in B.M. Schoenberg (ed.) *Bereavement Counselling: A Multidisciplinary Handbook.* Westport, CT: Greenwood Press.

Raphael, B. (1984) *The Anatomy of Bereavement.* London: Hutchinson.

Raphael, B. and Nunn, K. (1988) Counseling the bereaved. *Journal of Social Issues,* 44: 191–206.

Raphael, B., Middleton, W., Martinek, N. and Misso, V. (1993) Counseling and therapy of the bereaved, in M.S. Stroebe, W. Stroebe and R.O. Hansson, *Handbook of Bereavement*. Cambridge: Cambridge University Press.

Rees, W.D. and Lutkins, S.G. (1967) Mortality of bereavement. *British Medical Journal*, 4: 13–16.

Relf, M. (1997) How effective are volunteers in providing bereavement care? in F. De Como (ed.) *Proceedings of the 4th Congress of the European Association for Palliative Care* (6–9 December 1995). Barcelona: EAPC.

Relf, M. (1998) An evaluation of a bereavement service using trained volunteers. Paper presented at 'Advancing Scientific Care: A Scientific Conference to Celebrate Dame Cicely Saunders 80th Birthday'. June, London.

Richardson, R. (1988) *Death, Destitution and the Destitute*. London: Routledge.

Riches, G. and Dawson, P. (1997) Shoring up the walls of heartache: parental responses to the death of a child, in D. Field, J. Hockey and N. Small (eds) *Death, Gender and Ethnicity*. London: Routledge.

Robbins, R.A. (1992) Death competency: a study of hospice volunteers. *Death Studies*, 16: 557–69.

Robertson, J. (1953) *A Guide to the Film 'A Two-year-old Goes to Hospital'*. London: Tavistock Child Development Research Unit.

Robinson, S. (1992) The family with cancer. *European Journal of Cancer Care*, 1(2): 29–33.

Rosenblatt, P.C. (1993) Grief: the social context of private feelings, in M.S. Stroebe, W. Stroebe and R.O. Hansson (eds) *Handbook of Bereavement*. Cambridge: Cambridge University Press.

Rosenblatt, P.C. (1997) Grief in small-scale societies, in C.M. Parkes, P. Laungani and B. Young (eds) *Death and Bereavement Across Cultures*. London: Routledge.

Roskin, M. (1984) A look at bereaved parents. *Bereavement Care*, 3: 26–8.

Rotter, J.B. (1966) Generalised expectancies for internal versus external control of reinforcement. *Psychological Monographs*, 80: 1–28.

Rubin, S. (1984) Maternal attachment and child death: on adjustment, relationship and resolution. *Omega: Journal of Death and Dying*, 15(4): 347–52.

Rubin, S. (1993) The death of a child is forever: the life course impact of child loss, in M.S. Stroebe, W. Stroebe and R.O. Hansson (eds) *Handbook of Bereavement*. Cambridge: Cambridge University Press.

Sanders, C.M. (1981) Comparison of younger and older spouses in bereavement outcome. *Omega: Journal of Death and Dying*, 11: 217–32.

Sanders, C.M. (1983) Effects of sudden versus chronic illness death on bereavement outcome. *Omega: Journal of Death and Dying*, 11: 227–41.

Sanders, C.M. (1988) Risk factors in bereavement outcome. *Journal of Social Issues*, 44: 97–111.

Sanders, C.M. (1989) *Grief: The Mourning After*. Chichester: John Wiley & Sons.

Sanders, C.M. (1993) Risk factors in bereavement outcome, in M.S. Stroebe, W. Stroebe and R.O. Hansson (eds) *Handbook of Bereavement*. Cambridge: Cambridge University Press.

Sanders, C.M., Mauger, P.A. and Strong, P.A. (1985) *A Manual For The Grief Experience Inventory*. Palo Alto, CA: Consulting Psychologists Press.

Schwab, R. (1992) Effects of a child's death on the marital relationship: a preliminary study. *Death Studies*, 16: 141–54.

Segal, U.A. (1991) Cultural variables in Asian Indian families. *Families in Society*, 72(4): 233–42.

Selye, H. (1956) *The Stress of Life*. New York: McGraw-Hill.

Sherr, L. (ed.) (1995) *Grief and AIDS*. Chichester: John Wiley & Sons.

Shuchter, S.R. and Zisook, S. (1993) The course of normal grief, in M.S. Stroebe, W. Stroebe and R.O. Hansson (eds) *Handbook of Bereavement*. Cambridge: Cambridge University Press.

Silverman, P.R. (1970) The widow as a caregiver in a programme of preventive intervention with other widows. *Mental Hygiene*, 54: 540–7.

Silverman, P.R. (1986) *Widow to Widow*. New York: Springer Publishing Company.

Silverman, P.R., Nickman, S. and Worden, J.W. (1992) Detachment revisited: the child's reconstruction of a dead parent. *American Journal of Orthopsychiatry*, 62(4): 494–503.

Smith, C.R. (1982) *Social Work With the Dying and Bereaved*. London: Macmillan.

Smith, R.J. (1974) *Ancestor Worship in Contemporary Japan*. Stanford, CA: Stanford University Press.

Sque, M. and Payne, S. (1996) Dissonant loss: the experience of donor relatives. *Social Science and Medicine*, 43(9): 1359–70.

St Christopher's Hospice Information Service (1992) *Directory of Hospice Services in the UK and Ireland*. Sydenham: St Christopher's Hospice Information Service.

Stanners, C. (1987) The levers of change: a study of a change of goal in a voluntary organisation. Unpublished MA dissertation, Brunel University.

Stanworth, R. (1997) Spirituality, language and depth of reality. *International Journal of Palliative Nursing*, 3(1): 19–22.

Stewart, J. (1994) *Guidelines for Setting Up a Bereavement Service*. London: National Association of Bereavement Services.

Stokes, J., Wyer, S. and Crossley, D. (1997) The challenge of evaluating a child bereavement programme. *Palliative Medicine*, 11: 179–90.

Stroebe, M.S. (1992/3) Coping with bereavement: a review of the grief work hypothesis. *Omega: Journal of Death and Dying*, 26: 19–42.

Stroebe, M.S. (1997) From mourning and melancholia to bereavement and biography: an assessment of Walter's new model of grief. *Mortality*, 2(3): 255–62.

Stroebe, M.S. (1998) New directions in bereavement research: exploration of gender differences. *Palliative Medicine*, 12: 5–12.

Stroebe, M.S. and Schut, H. (1996) A model for coping with grief and its practical applications for the bereavement counsellor. Paper presented at the third St George's 'Dying, Death and Bereavement' conference, St George's Hospital medical school, London, 6 March.

Stroebe, M.S. and Schut, H. (1998) Culture and grief. *Bereavement Care*, 17(1): 7–10.

Stroebe, M.S. and Stroebe, W. (1983) Who suffers more? Sex differences in health risks of the widowed. *Psychological Bulletin*, 93: 279–301.

Stroebe, M.S. and Stroebe, W. (1987) *Bereavement and Health*. Cambridge: Cambridge University Press.

Stroebe, M.S., Stroebe, W. and Domittner, G. (1988) Bereavement research: an historical introduction. *Journal of Social Issues*, 44: 1–8.

Stroebe, M.S., Stroebe, W. and Hansson, R.O. (eds) (1993a) *Handbook of Bereavement*. Cambridge: Cambridge University Press.

Stroebe, M.S., Stroebe, W. and Hansson, R.O. (1993b) Bereavement research and theory: an introduction, in M.S. Stroebe, W. Stroebe and R.O. Hansson (eds) *Handbook of Bereavement*. Cambridge: Cambridge University Press.

Stroebe, W., Stroebe, M.S., Abakoumkin, G. and Schut, H. (1996) The role of loneliness and social support in adjustment to loss: a test of attachment versus stress theory. *Journal of Personality and Social Psychology*, 70(6): 1241–9.

Stuifbergen, A.K. (1990) Patterns of functioning in families with a chronically ill parent: an exploratory study. *Research in Nursing and Health*, 13: 35–44.

Sullivan, H.L. (1956) The dynamics of emotion, in H.L. Sullivan (ed.) *Clinical Studies in Psychiatry*. New York: Norton.

Taylor, L. (1983) *Mourning Dress: A Costume and Social History*. London: Allen & Unwin.

Torrie, M. (1987) *My Years with Cruse*. Richmond, VA: Cruse House.

Treacher, A. and Carpenter, J. (eds) (1984) *Using Family Therapy*. Oxford: Basil Blackwell.

Tutty, L.M. (1995) Theoretical and practical issues in selecting a measure of family functioning. *Research on Social Work Practice*, 5(1): 80–106.

Tyndall, N. (1993) *Counselling in the Voluntary Sector*. Buckingham: Open University Press.

Vachon, M.L.S. (1978) Motivation and stress experienced by those working with advanced cancer patients. *Death Education*, 2: 113–22.

Vachon, M.L.S. and Stylianos, S.K. (1988) The role of social support in bereavement. *Journal of Social Issues*, 44: 175–90.

Vachon, M.L.S., Freedman, K., Formo, A., Rogers, J. and Lyall, W.A.L. (1977) The final illness in cancer: the widow's perspective. *Canadian Medical Association Journal*, 117: 1151–4.

Vachon, M.L.S., Sheldon, A.R., Lancee, W.J. *et al.* (1982a) Correlates of enduring distress patterns following bereavement: social network, life situation and personality. *Psychological Medicine*, 12: 783–8.

Vachon, M.L.S., Rogers, J., Lyall, W.A.L. *et al.* (1982b) Predictors and correlates of adaptation to conjugal bereavement. *American Journal of Psychiatry*, 139: 998–1002.

Vafeiadou, S. (1997) The oncology setting: staff burnout, psychological symptomatology and death attitudes. Unpublished MSc dissertation, University of Southampton.

Van Gennep, A. (1965) *The Rites of Passage*. London: Routledge and Kegan Paul.

Vetere, A. and Gale, A. (1987) *Ecological Studies of Family Life*, Chichester: John Wiley & Sons.

Wallston, K.A., Wallston, B.S. and DeVellis, R. (1978) Development of the multidimensional health locus of control (MHLOC) scale. *Health Education Monographs*, 6(2): 161–70.

Walter, T. (1990) *Funerals and How to Improve Them*. London: Hodder.

Walter, T. (1994) *The Revival of Death*. London: Routledge.

Walter, T. (1996a) A new model of grief: bereavement and biography. *Mortality*, 1(1): 7–25.

Walter, T. (1996b) Bereavement models. *Progress in Palliative Care*, 4(1): 9–11.

Walter, T. (1997a) The ideology and organisation of spiritual care: three approaches. *Palliative Medicine*, 11: 21–30.

Walter, T. (1997b) Bereavement: a biographical approach. Paper presented at the '5th Congress of the European Association of Palliative Care', London, 11 September.

Wambach, J.A. (1985) The grief process as a social construct. *Omega: Journal of Death and Dying*, 16: 201–11.

Weiss, R.S. (1975) *Loneliness: The Experience of Emotional and Social Isolation*. Cambridge, MA: MIT Press.

Whippen, D.A. and Canellos, G.P. (1991) Burnout syndrome in the practice of oncology: results of a random survey of 1000 Oncologists. *Journal of Clinical Oncology*, 9: 1916–20.

Wikan, U. (1989) Managing the heart to brighten the face and soul: emotions in Balinese morality and health care. *American Ethnologist*.

Wilkes, E. (1993) Characteristics of hospice bereavement services. *Journal of Cancer Care*, 2: 183–9.

Worden, J.W. (1982) *Grief Counselling and Grief Therapy*. New York: Springer Publishing.

Worden, J.W. (1991) *Grief Counselling and Grief Therapy*, 2nd edn. New York: Springer Publishing.

Worden, J.W. and Silverman, P.R. (1996) Parental death and the adjustment of school-age children. *Omega*, 33(2): 91–103.

Wortman, C.B. and Silver, R.C. (1989) The myths of coping with loss. *Journal of Consulting and Clinical Psychology*, 57(3): 349–57.

Wymer, J. (1982) *The Palaeolithic Age*. Beckenham: Croom Helm.

Yasko, J.M. (1983) Variables which predict burnout experienced by oncology and clinical nurse specialists. *Cancer Nursing*, 6: 109–16.

Young, M. and Cullen, L. (1996) *A Good Death*. London: Routledge.

Young, M., Benjamin, B. and Wallis, C. (1963) The mortality of widowers. *The Lancet*, 2: 454–6.

Zisook, S. and DeVaul, R.A. (1985) Unresolved grief. *American Journal of Psychoanalysis*, 45: 370–9.

Index